WITHDRAWAL

SOCRATES

in the

BOARDROOM

SOCRATES

in the

BOARDROOM

Why Research Universities
Should Be Led by Top Scholars

AMANDA H. GOODALL

PRINCETON UNIVERSITY PRESS   PRINCETON AND OXFORD

To Andrew

A ship's crew which does not understand that the art of navigation demands a knowledge of the stars, will stigmatize a properly qualified pilot as a star-gazing idiot, and will prevent him from navigating.
—*Plato*

Research is an expression of faith in the possibility of progress. Research, especially academic research, is a form of optimism about the human condition.
—*Henry Rosovsky*

CONTENTS

Acknowledgments

Many people from around the world have provided me intellectual support and shown me kindness throughout this project. Scholars who were unknown to me have been prepared to read my papers and send me invaluable comments. Thank you.

I would especially like to thank three individuals who have given me so much encouragement: Ron Ehrenberg at Cornell University, Charles Oppenheim at Loughborough University, and Henry Rosovsky at Harvard. I have also received generous support from James Adams, Warren Bennis, Alan Bryman, Paula Marshall, Robert May, and Mark Taylor. This book grew out of my PhD thesis at the University of Warwick. I am indebted to my supervisors, David Wilson at Warwick, and Stephen Machin at University College London and the London School of Economics, and grateful also for the assistance I have received from Howard Thomas, Dean of Warwick Business School.

This work has been enhanced by the interview material from university leaders. I am extremely grateful to those who agreed to be interviewed, both in the United Kingdom and the United States—all of whom have little time to spare. They include: George Bain, Derek Bok, Glynis Breakwell, Robert Burgess, Yvonne Carter, Kim Clark, Ivor Crewe, Howard Davies, Anthony Giddens, Alan Gilbert, David Grant, Amy Gutmann, Patrick Harker, John Heilbron, John Hood, Jeremy Knowles (who sadly died in April 2008), Paul Nurse, Andrew Pettigrew, Henry Rosovsky, David Skorton, Lawrence Summers, Richard Sykes, Eric Thomas, Nigel Thrift, and Bill Wakeham. I am equally indebted to those I interviewed from professional service firms: Maurice Dwyer, Peter Oborn, Kieran Poynter, Graham Shuttleworth, and also Paul McGrath and John Silver, and finally, to those anonymous interviewees in the case study of a selection panel.

Thank you to Rose Batt, Fran Blau, Robert Frank, Kevin Hallock, Alice Isen, Kirabo Jackson, Larry Kahn, Darrie O'Connell, Robin Remick, and John Sipple who gave me useful comments while I was a research fellow in the School of Industrial and Labor Relations at Cornell University (where this book was mostly written). I am also thankful to Uschi Backes-Gellner, Josef Falkinger, Egon Franck, Andrea Schenker, Liliana Winkleman, and Rainer Winkleman at the University of Zurich (where the book was finished off). I was given helpful and encouraging comments on the first draft of this book from William Bowen and other anonymous referees—thank you.

Others who have given me helpful comments include Philip Altbach, Jon Baldwin, John Benington, Mary Blair, David Blanchflower, Lisa Boudreau, Sara Brailsford, Sue Bridgewater, G. D. A. Brown, Alison Browning, Richard Chait, Bruce Charlton, Cathy Charlton, Alison Cheevers, Andrew Clark, Simon Collinson, Megan Comfort, Rachel Condry, Scott Dacko, Rosemary Deem, Kate Dodd, Carol Douet, Chris Edgar, Dan Gilbert, Helen Goodall, Philip Goodall, Liam Graham, Paul Greatrix, Hugh Gregory, Keith Grint, Vin Hammersly, Mark Harrison, Jean Hartley, Judith Higgin, Diana Holton, Janice Isaac, Paula Jarzabkowski, John Leighfield, Kate Malleson, Robin Middlehurst, Sharun Mukand, Abhinay Muthoo, Dennis Novy, Brendan O'Leary, James Oswald, Reeve Parker, Simon Peatfield, Anita Phillips, Leah Popowich, Nick Powdthavee, Leah Rosovsky, Lucio Sarno, Sarah Shalgosky, Stephen Sharp, Michael Shattock, Swaran Singh, Ken Sloan, Mark Smith, Bridgette Sullivan-Taylor, William Swann, William Taylor, Larry Treanor, Michelle Tytherleigh, Claire Visser, Mary Visser, Michael Whitby, Gareth Williams, and Lyuba Zolotova.

I am also grateful to Warwick Business School (WBS) for the research award I received, and to Janet Biddle, Sheila Frost, Lindsey Marr, and the Marketing and Strategic Management Group at WBS for their support over the years, also to Debra Bennett, Katherine Branch, Nikki Muckle, and Lisa Wilberforce in Warwick's super-efficient research office. For access to data, thanks to the Association of Commonwealth Universities and the Higher Education Statistics Agency, and for generous financial support throughout this project, I am indebted to the Economic and Social Research Council (ESRC) in the United Kingdom.

I left school at sixteen with no qualifications. I turned up at the London School of Economics (LSE) at thirty-three having had a gap-decade or two. I am especially indebted to a number of people at LSE for giving me both the benefit of the doubt and a great education: John Carrier, Stan Cohen, David Downes, Jane Falkingham, Julian le Grand, Bob Pinker, Paul Rock, and Sally Sainsbury.

Big thanks also to my attentive, supportive (and humorous) editor Richard Baggaley and to others at Princeton University Press, including Peter Dougherty, Caroline Priday, Heath Renfroe, Kimberley Johnson, and Dawn Hall. I am enormously appreciative too for all the love, friendship, and red wine I have received from my fabulous friends, my wonderful family, old and new, and my canine comrade. Finally, it would not be a cliché to say that this book could not have been written without the generous encouragement and patience I have received from my partner, Andrew Oswald. It is to him, with love, that I dedicate this book.

PREFACE

THIS IS A BOOK about the leadership of experts. My focus is on heads of universities—although not exclusively so. I ask the question: does it matter to the performance of a research university if the president has been a highly cited scholar? Then, using evidence, I attempt to answer it. My conclusion is that better scholars make better leaders.

My research has benefited greatly from many insightful comments from academics and others around the world, for which I am extremely thankful. There is one claim, however, that is often raised with which I always take issue: it is the assertion that academics do not make good managers or leaders. This opinion, often stated vociferously, comes from a number of scholars, administrators, and those outside universities, including politicians, civil servants, and business people. The president of a powerful U.S. university has said it to me, and I have heard it from individuals who have barely stepped foot in a university, which implies it has reached folklore proportions. When I ask for evidence, faculty members will often tell anecdotal stories about a former department chair; and from those outside the academy, there appears to be a general belief that people clever enough to be academics must lack normal human organizational abilities.

Universities could be accused of being poor at training their faculty in management and leadership. In research universities, it is usual for departmental heads to rotate every few years, and it is common for a professor to walk—or be dragged—directly into the job with no prior instruction. But this is a different argument from the one I hear, that academics are somehow less able than those in other walks of life at managing or leading. I often respond to these claims by posing a scenario: imagine that one hundred nurses and the same number of lawyers, chefs, advertising executives, engineers, journalists, and academics are randomly selected. Will we find that one group or profession stands out as natural managers? Is it not more likely that management skills are learned through training and experience, and that the propensity to manage is, approximately, evenly distributed across all professions? (Leadership may be somewhat different.) Those at the tails of the distribution may fare less well. But I find it hard to accept that academics are, by some natural force, less adept. Universities are among society's oldest and most respected institutions. If scholars are so bad in these areas, why do universities do so well, often against odds like decreasing funds and more than occasional outside interference?

The business of research universities the world over is the same—research and teaching. I believe that the findings in this study can be generalized across borders. My work is almost solely on the executive heads of universities, commonly called presidents, vice chancellors, and rectors, among other titles. I view this position as the most important in a university. My data consist mainly of presidents, although I also interview a number of deans, and include a chapter on business schools, and one that looks at university boards. Nonacademic administrators perform an important role in universities. Indeed, they are the glue to which everything sticks. But I do not discuss these functions here.

The work uses quantitative and interview data. I view this book as being both academic and applied. I have tried to present the quantitative evidence simply, with accessible explanations, while also providing enough information to those more adept at statistics. My hope is that this work makes a contribution to the study of leadership, and to our understanding of research universities; and also, that the findings will be helpful to those who wish to hire university leaders—for example, governing boards and headhunters.

Finally, I would like to comment on the methodological approach I have adopted in this study. It is common for graduate students to be introduced to academe via a disciplinary passage, thus coming out to see the world through a specific theoretical and methodological lens. As a PhD student I adopted a different approach and am grateful to my doctoral supervisors for their support in this. I felt there was an interesting research question to be answered, and I have tried to choose the methodological tools accordingly. My intellectual home is in a business school and I view myself primarily as a management researcher; but I have drawn from other disciplines for assistance. In particular, I have found economics to be helpful, and I have also drawn from educationalists, and to a smaller degree from psychology.

SOCRATES

in the

BOARDROOM

CHAPTER ONE

THE ARGUMENT

AROUND THE YEAR 870, a bridge was built across the river Cam in England. In 1209, in that location, by then named Cambridge, one of the world's first universities was established. Nearly eight hundred years later, Cambridge University appointed its 344th and most recent president, or vice chancellor (VC),[1] Alison Richard. Richard is the first woman to lead Cambridge University. She is a distinguished anthropologist who spent her academic career at Yale University, from which in 2003 she left the position of provost to join Cambridge. Just a year later, in 2004, another long-standing English university installed its 270th vice chancellor, John Hood. Hood became the first head of Oxford University since the year 1230 to be elected to the vice chancellorship from outside the university's current academic body. Indeed Hood, a New Zealander, is not an academic. He spent most of his career in business.[2]

Why did Cambridge and Oxford choose two such different individuals to lead their ancient institutions?

The same year that Alison Richard boarded an eastbound jet, the Nobel Prize–winning biologist Paul Nurse left England for New York to become Rockefeller University's ninth president. He is not the only Nobel laureate to run a top American institution. David Baltimore, who stood down as president of the California Institute of Technology in 2006, is also a Nobel Prize winner, as is J. Michael Bishop, chancellor of the University of California, San Francisco. Indeed California has some of the most distinguished scholars in the world leading its universities. John Hennessy, at Stanford, is a prominent computer scientist; Robert Birgeneau, a Canadian who heads Berkeley, is a top physicist. At the University of California (UC), San Diego, Chancellor Marye Anne Fox is an eminent chemist, and at UC Irvine, the renowned atmospheric scientist Ralph Cicerone was chancellor until he left his position in 2005 to head the National Academy of Sciences. The University of California is arguably one of the best public university systems in the

---

[1] A vice chancellor is the principal academic and administrative officer or CEO, akin to a university president or rector. In this book the term *president* will normally be used to denote the head of a university, though other titles may also be referred to interchangeably.

[2] Interestingly, at the time of writing it was announced that John Hood would be replaced as head of Oxford University by Andrew Hamilton, another former provost from Yale University.

world (although it is currently enduring major financial cutbacks by the state government). The State of California is home to many great institutions. The success of UC is often attributed to its founding president, Clark Kerr, who was himself a distinguished economist.

Could it be that the high achievement of California's universities today is explained partially by the academic standards introduced by Kerr, and partially by the legacy left by a string of noted scholars who have led many of California's top institutions?

This book asks the question: is there a relationship between university performance and leadership by an accomplished researcher? The central conclusion, supported by evidence, is that top scholars should lead research universities.

WHY IT MATTERS WHO LEADS RESEARCH UNIVERSITIES

My underlying assumption is that the world needs outstanding research universities, and, therefore, that it matters who leads them.[3] Most importantly, there appears to be a positive externality effect on economic growth from the amount of money that governments invest in public or university research. This happens through spillover effects that research universities generate. Such spillovers occur when the creativity or knowledge in an individual or organization spreads outward, resulting in the growth of more creativity and knowledge. In short, good ideas rub off on other people. Research universities produce intellectual externalities of many kinds (and also nonintellectual externalities like jobs). Their most important outputs are inventions and ideas.[4] Economic growth, at a national and regional level, can be directly traced back to governments' investment in research and development. A growing number of studies suggest that university research is critical to industry, R&D, and the development of new technologies, and also to the creation and expansion of new firms and start-ups. There is also a strong correlation between the location of top scientists and the establish-

---

[3] This is not to suggest that other higher education institutions are less important, only that these are what I know. In this book I use the Carnegie Foundation for the Advancement of Teaching's report, "A Classification of Institutions of Higher Education," to define a research university. The report states that research universities offer a full range of undergraduate programs, are committed to graduate education through the doctorate, give high priority to research, and consider research capability as a primary qualification for appointment, promotion, and tenure of faculty members (www.carnegiefoundation.org/classifications).

[4] Teaching students is also an important output; however, the evidence suggests that a university education tends to benefit the individual student more than society as a whole (see Krueger and Lindahl [2001] and Oreopoulos [2007]). For this reason I believe that undergraduate students (graduate students are different) should not be heavily subsidized by the state, given the enormous financial benefit of a degree to individuals later in life. But generous scholarships for those who cannot afford fees should be readily available.

ment of biotechnology firms.[5] In short, the social return from academic research appears to be high.

There are other benefits from the research output of universities. They are subtler. How is it possible to quantify the value of constant discoveries in medicine, physics, chemistry, or psychiatry, or the social science findings about the positive effects of education and the negative effects of poverty and discrimination? How much have we learned from history about civilization? What of the aesthetic and creative contributions of the arts and humanities? And on, and on. Moreover, and importantly, universities seek to develop and disseminate ideas independently from the state and pressure groups. This objectivity has proved essential in, for example, uncovering the phenomenon of climate change, which has been subject to much diverse political interpretation. All these are among the unaccounted externalities and spillovers of universities.

On the subject of the best form of university leadership and governance, interest has grown around the world. This is because the sector has become global and increasingly competitive. Major changes have taken place in institutions of higher education, and subsequently in the role and responsibilities of their leaders.[6] This research is motivated in part by the recent emphasis on "managerialism" in universities and more widely in the public sectors in a number of countries. There has been a suggestion that managers as leaders may be preferable. This book argues that in universities, where the majority of employees are expert workers, having a leader who is also an expert is likely to be beneficial to the institution's long-term performance. The alternative argument takes the form: what a leader in a university or knowledge-based sector needs is primarily high managerial ability allied merely to some acceptable minimum level of technical ability. By contrast, what the later data in this study suggest is a fairly smooth relationship between the leader's level of scholarship and a university's quality. The greater is the first, the greater is the second.

The role of university presidents and their education and career history has attracted interest in previous important research,[7] but relatively little

[5] For the influence of human capital externalities on economic growth see Lucas (1988). For the economic effects of university or public research, see Adams (1990) and Adams and Clemmons (2008); Anselin, Varga, and Acs (1997, 2000); Basu, Fernald, and Shapiro (2001); Basu et al. (2003); Cohen, Nelson, and Walsh (2002); Aghion et al. (2005); Aghion (2006); Stuen (2007); and Bramwell and Wolfe (2008). For a link between the location of top scientists and increases in the number of biotech firms, see Zucker et al. (1998). On how the location of university graduates increases salaries for those less educated, see Moretti (2004). For a link with top scholars and size-of-research-team effect on scientific outputs and influence, see Adams et al. (2005).

[6] See for example, Bowen and Shapiro (1998); Bargh et al. (2000); Bok (2003); Bornstein (2003); and Shapiro (2005).

[7] Szreter (1968); Halsey and Trow (1971); Cohen and March (1974); Taylor (1986); Tierney (1988, 1989); Bensimon (1989); Rosovsky (1991); Middlehurst (1993); Bowen

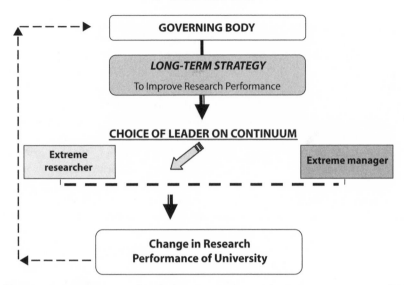

Figure 1-1. Appointment of a scholar on a continuum between extreme researcher and extreme manager

attention has been given specifically to the scholarly background of academic leaders. This question, of whether or not to appoint a major scholar, has circulated around universities in the United States and Europe for a number of years. In principle, every president's Search Committee grapples with the issue. Yet there appears to be no consensus.

To my knowledge, this is the first study to address this question empirically. Given the centrality of research performance in many institutional mission statements—expressed through the quality of research produced and the scholarly reputation of staff—it seems logical to turn to the academic ability of their leaders.

Figure 1.1 presents the central argument in a schematic model that links the appointment of a scholar with the performance of a university. It suggests that if a governing body has decided upon a strategy of raising or maintaining the research performance of their university, then hiring a leader who is a scholar may be the right choice. The diagram oversimplifies a complicated process but serves to illustrate the point and to introduce the main conceptual claim.

In this book, I draw from four separate datasets. My research starts by looking at who currently heads the world's top 100 universities. I then focus on deans in the top business schools. Next I explore whether the characteris-

and Shapiro (1998); Bargh et al. (2000); Ehrenberg (2002, 2004); Brodie and Banner (2005); and Keohane (2006).

TABLE 1.1
Interviews with University Leaders

U.S. UNIVERSITIES

Derek Bok, Former President, Harvard
Kim Clark, Dean, Harvard Business School
Amy Gutmann, President, U of Pennsylvania
Patrick Harker, Dean, Wharton School
John Heilbron, Former Vice Chancellor, Berkeley
Jeremy Knowles, Former Dean, Harvard
Paul Nurse, President, Rockefeller U
Henry Rosovsky, Former Dean, Harvard
David Skorton, President, Cornell
Lawrence Summers, President, Harvard
Shirley Tilghman*, President, Princeton

UK UNIVERSITIES

George Bain, Former Vice Chancellor, Queen's U, Belfast
Glynis Breakwell, Vice Chancellor, Bath U
Bob Burgess, Vice Chancellor, Leicester U
Yvonne Carter, Dean, Warwick Medical School
Ivor Crewe, Vice Chancellor, Essex U
Howard Davies, Director, LSE
Anthony Giddens, Former Director, LSE
Alan Gilbert, President, Manchester U
David Grant, Vice Chancellor, Cardiff U
John Hood, Vice Chancellor, Oxford U
Andrew Pettigrew, Dean, Bath School of Management
Richard Sykes, Rector, Imperial
Eric Thomas, Vice Chancellor, Bristol
Nigel Thrift, Vice Chancellor, Warwick U
Bill Wakeham, Vice Chancellor, Southampton U

tics of a leader in position today can tell us about the future success of their institution. Finally, using interview data from twenty-six university leaders in the United States and the United Kingdom, I present possible explanations for why better scholars may make better leaders. Interview material with presidents will appear throughout the book to illustrate points about leadership in universities. Table 1.1 above lists the heads of universities I met with.

It is important to emphasize early that scholarship will not be viewed here as a proxy for either management experience or leadership skills. An "expert" leader must have expertise in areas other than scholarship. Also, it should not be assumed that all outstanding researchers will inevitably go on to make good managers or leaders. Before their step to the top position, most university presidents have gained management experience as provosts, pro–vice chancellors or deans, or by running major research centers or labs. This was the case with virtually all of the four hundred leaders examined in this study. Moreover, to head up an academic department or school, one must first be a senior member of the faculty—usually a full tenured professor. Tenure is only granted after extensive publications have been acquired. Thus, scholarship is already a prerequisite of leadership in research universities. The book's concerns go beyond this basic point.

In this study I focus on research performance, because it is research quality that top universities prioritize. As suggested above, career advancement is reliant on scholarly productivity, namely publications. That is not to say that brilliant teaching is unimportant but that it alone will not usually lead to promotion in most research universities. This situation may differ in colleges and universities that prioritize teaching.

There is a link between teaching and research. The material taught to students has come from research. Interestingly, there is somewhat limited evidence that better researchers also make better teachers. A relationship has been shown to exist between a university's success in the UK Research Assessment Exercise (RAE) and the standard of its teaching instruction, as established by scores obtained in Teaching Quality Assessment (TQA). TQA scores correlate highly with RAE scores.[8] In other words, those institutions that perform best in research tend also to obtain the highest teaching scores.[9]

Henry Rosovsky contemplates the link between research and teaching, and suggests: "Research, especially academic research, is a form of optimism about the human condition . . . Persons who have faith in progress and therefore possess an intellectually optimistic disposition—that is, teacher-scholars—are probably interesting and better professors. They are less likely to present their subjects in excessively cynical or reactionary terms."[10]

Rosovsky also makes the point that teaching the same subject for years is likely to lead to boredom or burnout. Being a researcher not only keeps the

[8] Shattock (2003).
[9] I recently analyzed data on the teaching scores of faculty in a North American university with a view to addressing this question (are good researchers also good teachers?). As a first step I was sent only data on academics who received the highest teaching scores and who received the lowest scores. The sample included around fifty faculty members, approximately half in each group. Immediately it was clear that those in the "bad teachers" group were overwhelmingly scientists—mostly chemists and physicists; whereas, the opposite was true for those in the "good teachers" group, which was dominated by faculty from the humanities and social sciences. This is interesting, if not unexpected, given what we know about students' preferences for these subjects in North America and Europe. To attempt to answer the original question, we will need to control for discipline.
[10] Rosovsky (1991, p. 89).

information fresh and up to date, but also keeps the teacher from "falling asleep at the very mention of the assignment."[11]

Thus, those who are committed to research are possibly also more passionate about the topic, and therefore may be better educators. But the jury is still out on this question.

THE KEY ARGUMENTS IN THE BOOK

It is hoped that the evidence presented in this book will inform those involved in the selection of university presidents. The mission, or core business, of research universities tends not to differ across countries, nor to change through time. It is research and teaching. The discussion about why better scholars might make a difference to university performance is also explored using interview material with twenty-six leaders in universities.[12]

The main propositions in this book are:

1. Research universities should be led by individuals who have been accomplished scholars in their academic careers. It is not sufficient for university presidents to have management skills alone.
2. A president's appropriate level of scholarship will depend on where the university currently is—in terms of its research ambitions or position in rankings—and where it wants to be. How good should a scholar-leader be? A possible rule of thumb is that the prior research success of a leader should be equal to or better than the top 10 percent of faculty in the institution that he or she is to run.
3. University presidents need power if they are to lead. Presidents in the United States in general have more authority than those in European universities. Great Britain is moving in the direction of the United States—many heads can now select their own top management team. However, in other European countries, important strategic decisions are still being made by committees elected by large numbers of faculty.
4. Organizations linked to university policy-making or funding should also only be led by noted scholars. These would include government agencies like the National Science Foundation in the United States, the Higher Education Funding Councils in Britain and the European Union, the UK's Economic and Social Research Council, and trusts and foundations.
5. The reasons why presidents should be able scholars are fourfold:

[11] Ibid., p. 90.

[12] I have allowed myself room to expand upon ideas thrown up by the quantitative and qualitative findings, and I am informed by my own professional experience of having worked in an administrative capacity with university leaders over a number of years.

    a. Scholars are more *credible* leaders. A president who is a researcher will gain greater respect from academic colleagues and appear more legitimate. Legitimacy extends a leader's power and influence.

    b. Being a top scholar provides a leader with a deep understanding or *expert knowledge* about the core business of universities. This informs a president's decision-making and strategic priorities.

    c. The president sets the quality threshold in a university, and the bar is raised when an accomplished scholar is hired. Thus, a *standard bearer* has first set the standard that is to be enforced.

    d. A president who is a researcher sends a *signal* to the faculty that the leader shares their scholarly values, and that research success in the institution is important. It also transmits an external signal to potential academic hires, donors, alumni, and students.

6. The notion of leadership introduced in this book builds upon the idea that a leader's expert knowledge—about the core business of an organization—informs his or her decision-making in a way that has not been sufficiently studied. My central argument is that where expert knowledge is the key factor that characterizes an organization, it is expert knowledge that should also be key in the selection of its leader.

SETTING THE SCENE

Leaders matter. Much empirical work exposing the link between leaders and performance has emerged recently. Economists have shown in a number of settings that CEOs can substantially affect the profitability of firms. Similarly, the identities of particular leaders of nation-states have been linked to nations' later growth rates.[13] Central to my arguments about leadership is

---

[13] Bertrand and Schoar (2003) demonstrate that CEO fixed effects are correlated with firms' profitability. Their study is important because it suggests that individuals can shape outcomes. Jones and Olken (2005) examine the case of national leaders. By using, as a natural experiment, fifty-seven parliamentarians' deaths, and economic growth data on many countries between the years 1945 and 2000, the authors trace linkages between nations' leaders and nations' growth rates. The authors reject "the deterministic view . . . where leaders are incidental." Work by Bennedsen, Pérez-González, and Wolfenzon (2007) spans these two earlier papers by establishing, in Danish data, that the death of a CEO, or a close family member, is strongly correlated with a later decline in firm profitability. This, again, seems to confirm that leaders matter to the performance of organizations. Theoretical explorations of leadership are offered by Hermalin (1998, 2007), who focuses on the incentives leaders used to induce followers to follow; by Majumdar and Mukand (2007), who construct a model in which a key role is played by followers' willing to put their faith in their leader; and by Dewan and Myatt (2008), who concentrate on the role played by a leader's ability, and willingness, to communicate clearly to followers.

the way universities are categorized. Research universities should, I argue, be viewed as knowledge-centered organizations. Their core business is that of generating understanding of the world, by research, and disseminating it through their publishing and teaching. This depends on the knowledge of experts, not generalists. In many countries, universities have traditionally been seen as an extension of the public sector. The role of leadership in the public and private sectors is often looked upon differently. This, I believe, is a mistake. The exact sector is largely irrelevant to the key issue; instead, it is the core business that should determine, or at least contribute to, the identification of appropriate institutional heads.

Professional service firms—such as law, accounting, and architecture firms—are somewhat akin to universities. Professionals are treated as "autonomous competent individuals"[14] who, on the whole, manage themselves. This does not mean that administrative and management support is unnecessary, only that management functions should not impinge too directly on professionals.[15] With this in mind I emphasize professionalism over managerialism as essential for leadership in universities —a setting where leaders' technical ability can be measured reasonably objectively.

EXPERTS VERSUS MANAGERS

What matters is scholarship not just
management. We should take
management for granted.[16]

The attention paid in this book to a leader's technical ability sits in contrast to recent emphasis on the managerial skills of university presidents. Over the past two decades, politicians in a number of countries have sought to introduce a business or "managerialist" culture into the public sector, often called "new managerialism" or its less ideological counterpart, "new public management."[17] In one country, the United Kingdom, universities have been exposed to a range of management practices, and academics have experienced the pressures of external accountability and a continuous cycle of performance monitoring and quality audits. The shift to managerialism in

[14] Handy (1984), in Middlehurst and Elton (1992, p. 225).

[15] Handy (1984); Maister (1993).

[16] In correspondence with a former UK vice chancellor who wished to remain anonymous.

[17] For "new managerialism" see Clarke and Newman (1994, 1997); for "new public management" see Hood (2000). In UK universities see Deem (1998); Deem and Brehony (2005); and Deem, Hillyard, and Reed (2007) and Pollitt (1993). Charlton (2002), following Power (1997) argues that the ubiquitous use of audit, accountability, and quality measures in the United Kingdom are because of the influence of accountancy firms. Whereas in Germany, he argues, an engineering culture dominates management processing.

Britain was initiated by former Prime Minister Margaret Thatcher and bed-ded down by former PM Tony Blair.[18] In a review of the Blair era in the journal *Nature*, Robert May, former chief scientific adviser to the UK gov-ernment, expressed fears that the "extreme growth of bureaucracy—too often masquerading as accountability," has ballooned out of all necessity, and created too many "conscientious administrators who hold meetings and send out forms to be filled in."[19] The suggestion is that the managerial sys-tems introduced and monitored by civil servants have become means in themselves, rather than a means to an end.

University administrators can at times also become overly focused on sys-tems that tend to suit staff more than the faculty they are there to support. It is unlikely to be beneficial for universities if the time of scientists and other scholars, whose research is vital to the success of intuitions, is diverted toward bureaucratic functions. Also, a distinguished academic is unlikely to remain at a university that overburdens him or her with paperwork and red tape. If a top researcher heads a university, should we expect greater sensitiv-ity about the administrative demands on faculty? Their shared experience and values might suggest so.

In many countries governments have extended their influence inside uni-versities. Consequently, universities have become less autonomous, academ-ics' influence has weakened, and, importantly, trust on both sides has de-clined. In America and Britain, public universities have witnessed increased bureaucratic and managerial interventions, which have been coupled with cuts in financial support from government. The views of one long-standing UK university president interviewed for this research are interesting:

> Since the Thatcher years, and then into Blair's period, universities have been condemned for being badly managed places; as if they are run by amateurs. I completely disagree and in fact I see it as insulting. I believe that the corporate sector has many more failures and also corruption and cover-ups. Don't get me wrong, I think the corporate sector has many things to teach us, particularly in the area of finance and project management, for example. But these can be bought in. They do not need to reside in senior positions.

[18] The late Martin Trow, a distinguished Berkeley scholar and author on educational matters, viewed the changes under Thatcher and later New Labour as "draconian" (Trow [2005]). But, "even more surprising," he suggests, "was the feeble response of the academic community to these policies, which, whatever their wisdom, were not friendly to an auton-omous university or academic community" (2005, p. 5). Trow also accuses the Committee of Vice Chancellors and Principals (CVCP now named Universities UK) as having been a peculiarly weak body over the whole of this half-century. Equally strange, he argues, was the response of the governing boards of universities that played almost no role in the changes in higher education, nor in their defense. See also Barnett (1988), Neave (1988), Jenkins (1995), and Greatrix (2005).

[19] May (2007, p. 28).

If we have not been efficient then I would like to see some evidence in terms of outputs. We have successfully educated a huge number of graduates, and for very little money. UK universities are the second most-cited after the United States, we have a massive share of the overseas market, and indeed many European countries are trying to emulate our system.

In the United States it has become somewhat more common for politicians to take over as presidents of state universities.[20] Arguably, this also reflects an attitude that universities can be led by individuals who, on the face of it, know nothing about academe or research. That state politicians are in some cases becoming presidents may be influenced by the salary the job commands. Some may view the position as a convenient place to put those who are no longer in office. State universities in the United States are also under financial pressure, and governing boards may view the appointment of a politician as useful when negotiating with government. I surmise, however, that the future of those institutions, especially in terms of maintaining research quality, will be more uncertain under the leadership of non-academics.

In the UK a milestone in the change of official attitude toward university leaders came in a government-sponsored document, the Jarratt Report, which both predicted and advocated that university vice chancellors should be hired because of their managerial qualities as opposed to their collegial authority.[21]

This book attempts to reconnect leadership with the core business of research universities—that of scholarship. This is not to ignore the importance of management systems, or the need to run organizations efficiently and offer the best service possible to faculty, staff, and students. Partly for this reason, there may be a case for privatizing universities. U.S. private universities are among the world's best, both in terms of research output and, in my experience, being efficiently run.[22]

---

[20] Martin Meehan, a long-time congressman, recently became president of the University of Massachusetts at Lowell. Bob Kerrey, former Nebraska senator, is the president of the New School, a University in New York. David Boren, former senator from Oklahoma, is president of the University of Oklahoma; and Bruce Benson, a former oilman and Republican activist, is head of the University of Colorado. Michael Garrison, a former political lobbyist, was president of West Virginia University for just one year, having to resign in June 2008 because of a political scandal. The University of Ottawa, in Canada, has also recently appointed a former politician as president.

[21] The Jarratt Report was commissioned by the UK government in 1985.

[22] Some people view the idea of private universities as inherently more inequitable. However, because of government restrictions on student fees in the United Kingdom, undergraduates are not charged a fee close to the actual costs of an undergraduate education. Therefore, overseas students are being relied upon to fill the financial gap. This means that not only are many excellent British and European students being denied undergraduate places at the best UK universities in subjects most in demand by international students,

Many of the leaders I interviewed were clear that management and leadership are different. The literature suggests that the former is about maintaining systems and instituting controls, and managers are seen as accepting the status quo. Organizational leaders, meanwhile, look at the bigger picture; they are more directly involved with strategy and also organizational change.[23] As suggested, the qualitative data appear to support this; among the twenty-six leaders in U.S. and UK universities interviewed for this book, the majority, when I asked them to describe the most important element of their job, emphasized leadership over management. The comments of one president illustrate this view:

> Leadership and management are profoundly different. I set goals for the university in discussion with colleagues. My aim is to create the best environment for academics.

Additionally, a number of university leaders interviewed stated that a president can buy in administrative and managerial expertise where he or she feels lacking:

> The chief function of a university president is leadership. Leadership is most important—not management or finance, these can be hired in.

On the point made in the book's preface, about how managerial talent is distributed somewhat evenly among the population, a former U.S. dean makes an interesting observation:

> A fair percentage of faculty are good managers with innate skills. In many ways this is akin to any profession because there will always be some who are better at leadership and management than others. I don't think academics are any different from others in this way. Being a dean at X is like being a CEO of a half-billion business ensuring it runs effectively. All faculty salaries are set by the dean. The position is somewhat similar to running a large law firm.

The distinction between managers and leaders may be especially important in universities—and other knowledge-based organizations—because of the

---

but also that British higher education is being subsidized by overseas students, many of whom come from developing countries. This system seems both inequitable and dishonest because the students who fail to get into in-demand courses are not being told why, nor are they being offered a place at an international rate they may choose to pay. It also does not seem right that a rich country like the United Kingdom is charging African or Thai students twice the fees of those in Europe. Around 12 percent of UK parents send their children to private schools costing on average £10,000 ($18,000) a year. It might be pertinent, therefore, to ask why students from these same families are paying less for a three-year university education.

[23] Zalznik (1977); Bennis and Nanus (1985); Bennis (1989); Kotter (1988, 1990); Middlehurst and Elton (1992).

technical ability required by those who lead scholars, experts, and professionals. Although all leaders will have management experience, most managerial and service functions will reside with highly specialized staff, for example registrars, directors of human resources, finance, and IT who are experts in these fields.

Much emphasis in the leadership literature, and the real world, has been placed on the idea of the charismatic leader. In contrast, and following others, the focus here is first on the context or organization, not on the individual.[24] Institutional heads must always have managerial experience and some minimum level of leadership talent. Being an expert, or a top researcher, is a necessary but not a sufficient condition for being a good leader. To succeed in any organization this is, of course, normally the case. I argue that it is also important to establish what level of *technical expertise* about the core business an individual should hold as a prerequisite to other factors. For example, the head, or chief of the Air Staff, of the Air Force will first have served some required period as an officer, normally a pilot, and may also have seen active duty. The head of a school has usually spent an amount of time as a teacher; and the CEO of a car manufacturer typically knows something about the industry because he or she has spent time in it.

The United Kingdom's *Financial Times* newspaper made this point about universities in 2008 in an article by Sir Richard Sykes, head of Imperial College London—one of the United Kingdom's top research universities. Prior to joining Imperial he was CEO of GlaxoSmithKline, a UK drug company with a $45 billion turnover (reported in their 2007 annual review). Although Sykes came from industry, he was actively involved in pharmaceutical research earlier in his career; consequently, he has a distinguished publishing record. The piece in the *Financial Times* reads:

> One of Britain's most respected academic heads has warned universities against appointing business people to the top post—even though he is himself a former CEO. Sir Richard Sykes, rector of Imperial College, London, told the *Financial Times* that putting a business person in charge was "easy to say and difficult to do." He cited the example of Oxford University, where John Hood, vice-chancellor, became locked in a bitter battle with dons over how to run the institution.[25]

This issue of whether business people should lead universities will be discussed later in chapter 5.

---

[24] Following Fiedler (1967); Bass (1985, 1990); Pettigrew (1985, 1990); Bennis (1989); Leavy and Wilson (1994); Bryman, Stephens, and Campo (1996); Khurana (2002); and others.

[25] *Financial Times*, October 29, 2007, p. 2.

THE BEST AMONG EQUALS

In the influential book on presidents, *Leadership and Ambiguity* published in 1974, Michael Cohen and James March describe the position of university head as leading in an "organized anarchy." This arises, they argue, in organizations commonly described as collegiate, where a leader is the first among equals. Without a hierarchical structure, Cohen and March suggest, leadership is at best vague and at worst an illusion.

Their view has been challenged. In particular, many question the notion that universities are nonhierarchical, pointing out that they use traditional organizational charts depicting a clear chain of command, akin to most private enterprises.[26] In Henry Rosovsky's introduction to his informative book *The University: An Owner's Manual*, he writes, "universities are institutions that love hierarchies and distinctions at least as much as the military."[27] The same might be said of professional service firms where, again, a similar misconception about hierarchy is often propagated. While law and accounting firms may have flatter organizational structures than most manufacturing companies, they are still run along traditional bureaucratic lines with promotion through a hierarchy.[28]

The structure of research universities has altered comparatively little over the hundreds of years they have existed, which is also at odds with Cohen and March's notion of ambiguity. Unlike many other types of organizations—banks, for example—universities have demonstrated unusual stability.[29] They have adapted to changes in the world while maintaining "business as usual," often with reduced funding. This line of argument is consistent with a comment made by one of the university presidents who was interviewed for this book; notably, he is from a nonacademic background.

> There is less freedom in a university. The strategic degrees of freedom are restricted. It is more difficult to change the course—the outputs are always going to be about the same.

Arguably, there have been changes in the role of university president that reflect on the one hand a globalized world, and on the other, expanding or shrinking markets, altered funding mechanisms, technological advances, enhanced competition, and so on. But the core business of a research university does not change. Even proclamations about the decline of "brick" and the rise of "click universities" hailed during the dot.com explosion of the late 1990s, proved to be incorrect. In Britain, the government lost

---

[26] See Middlehurst and Elton (1992) and Hammond (2004).
[27] Rosovsky (1991, p. 18). Henry Rosovsky was Dean of the Faculty of Arts and Sciences at Harvard University for eleven years.
[28] Maister (1993).
[29] Birnbaum (1988, 1992).

£50 million ($90 million) on its failed e-University project,[30] and many commercial online education companies, for example UNext.com, were forced by the early 2000s to alter their business model. Despite the sums of money spent on new pedagogical and technical innovations, traditional lectures and seminars continue.

POWER AND UNIVERSITY PRESIDENTS

Universities are important, and therefore so are those who lead them. Because leaders are not randomly assigned to organizations, measuring the effects of individuals on organizational performance is a challenge. Nevertheless, the quantitative analyses in chapter 4 attempt this. Another approach is to ask leaders how much power they have. I did this; specifically, I asked presidents: "whose role do you believe it is to write or construct the strategy for the university?" There was little or no hesitation among respondents, who, with few exceptions, stated that it was the responsibility of the president or vice chancellor. A number of authors argue that presidents need power if they are to successfully lead a university. Similarly, an institution that has too much "democracy" can become impotent. The decline of many European universities is attributed partially to their diffused decision-making processes—specifically, decision-making by elected committees. Interestingly, some scholars have suggested that university leaders with possibly the most direct powers reside in some of the best schools in the world, for example, Ivy League institutions, Stanford, and Caltech.[31]

One headhunter, who has been involved in the recruitment of a number of vice chancellors in Britain, believes that university chiefs may have more power than those at the helm in other industries. He said:

> There is no doubt that leaders have an enormous amount of power in universities—more than in many other organizations where the long-term strategy is firmly laid out. For example, in the civil service, or at the other extreme in Asda/Wal-Mart where the leader is a motivator for the "troops" but has very little say about the strategy of the business. That is all mapped out long before in somewhere like Ohio.[32]

What do university leaders say about it? A representative sample of interviewees' accounts are presented (there is not the space to include all statements on this topic). The comments of a former U.S. president are interesting:

[30] See the *Guardian* newspaper, June 23, 2004.
[31] On the subject of power and democracy see Rosovsky (1991), Trow (1999), and Kerr (2001). On university strategy see Jarzabkowski (2005).
[32] In fact Wal-Mart's headquarters are in Arkansas.

The background of presidents is most intriguing. Though 80% of their day may be spent undertaking a range of activities, the overall direction needs to be decided upon and led by the president. The president is often the only one who has the big-picture perspective about his or her university. If you devolve decision-making too far down you lose control, particularly of the academic direction.

Three UK vice chancellors stress that it is their responsibility to develop university strategy:

> The vice chancellor sets the agenda and tone—this is where you make a difference. The VC is the only person who can ask "Where are we going? What is our strategy?" No one else can do that. The VC can articulate the university's ambition.

A second vice chancellor makes the point that it is down to her to make the final decision:

> I determine the shape of strategy. Debates will emerge out of the top team but it is the responsibility of the president to finally say yes or no about an area of strategy. The buck stops with me.

A third UK head stresses the leader's responsibility as differentiated from that of committees:

> The final draft of the strategy has to come off the VC's PC. It is the role of the VC to put it together and then to get it approved and negotiate the details. It is not the job of any committee.

Finally, a similar comment is made by a U.S. president:

> I am very involved with the nuts and bolts of deciding the overall strategic direction of [my university]. I also decide the policy level direction.

Within my interviews, the degree of congruence on this topic is striking. Whether the sample of university leaders merely thinks that they write the strategy, compared to whether they actually do, cannot be dealt with properly here. However, if all university heads communicate in interview that they are responsible, it seems reasonable to believe them. Seemingly, leaders are appointed to make decisions, direct the institution, and take the fall when things do not work out. This explains why they usually receive the highest salary in their organizations. If governance mechanisms are functioning properly, powerful heads are, I believe, good for universities (governing boards are discussed further in chapter 6).

SELECTING THE TOP MANAGEMENT TEAM

Another of the powers bestowed on university heads is the right to hire top team members. The issue of top team selection is of particular importance to my research; this is because in the quantitative data in this book I focus on university presidents—on their influence as leaders. Arguably, members of the top team share executive responsibilities, but if deputies, deans, and key administrators are normally selected by leaders, then it may be fair to treat the team as an extension of the leaders who hired them.[33] Also, if a president has picked a dean it is likely that he or she will demonstrate loyalty and, in general, adhere to the wishes of the head. This allegiance, or collective responsibility, presumably explains some of what makes top management teams successful.

There are a number of tiers of leadership in research universities. Below presidents are provosts, pro–vice chancellors and other deputy heads, senior administrative staff, and leaders of key strategic units, such as deans of schools or faculties. For a leader to execute strategies and extend his or her influence, it matters whom she or he selects as provosts and pro–vice chancellors. Again, this tends to differ between the United States and Europe. It is normal for university presidents in American institutions to choose top team members and make other important hires. Almost all of the UK vice chancellors in my study complained that they had to first change or adapt the selection process within their own institution after they took over. Thus, in UK research universities, power to select top management teams is slowly following the U.S. example by shifting toward presidents.[34] The traditional European approach has been appointment through a process of faculty elections. This practice has been criticized because it substantially weakens presidential powers, inhibits organizational change, and favors the status quo.[35]

As one former U.S. dean said:

> I am strongly opposed to faculty making the selection of provosts or presidents, and generally I am against the notion of democracy.

A UK vice chancellor interviewed for this study explained he had experienced this kind of problem. He told me he had been chosen by the selection

[33] The top management team (TMT) has been widely covered in the literature on strategic leadership, initially through the work of Hambrick and Mason (1984) in upper echelons theory. Emphasis has tended to focus on top team members; in particular, how TMT characteristics influence organizational strategy and performance. However, it is the leader or CEO who normally selects the TMT, and, therefore, it could be argued that the top team should, on average, be viewed as an extension of the leader's influence. This, I believe, has been insufficiently covered in the TMT literature.

[34] It is more common for heads of New UK Universities, (those established from polytechnics after 1992) to have direct powers to select top teams.

[35] Rosovsky (1991).

committee to lead the university because of a strategy he presented in interview. When he took over as leader there were two pro–vice chancellors, or deputy leaders, in situ. The vice chancellor described in interview how his plans, that formed part of his original strategy, failed to be implemented because of the incumbent deputies. He explained that he had been powerless to do anything until their tenure was complete—he could not sack them. Only then could he engage in the process of selecting their successors. He eventually changed the way deputies are appointed. The comment below is from that leader:

> I had Pro–Vice Chancellors [PVCs] in place when I started; two of them blocked me from doing anything for 2 years. PVCs were appointed by Senate that had 200 members when I arrived. The system is not right in the United Kingdom. It is far too difficult to select our own top team.

This view is repeated by a second VC:

> PVCs are elected by Senate who make nominations. I think it is madness that a VC cannot select his or her own top team. I do now have some input through consultation—and I almost always get who I want. I did put my own non-academic administrators in place though, some of whom I appointed from the private sector.

Some UK heads negotiated the power to select top team members as part of their contract. This was true in the case of an experienced leader who was asked to take over the reins of a weak and struggling university:

> They all went! I introduced new PVCs, COO, registrar, etc.

This sentiment is reflected in the statement of another two UK heads:

> The VC now has total say on who gets the job [of PVC]. Faculty do not have any input.

And:

> I now appoint all the PVCs and deans, but I had to change the structure to do this. Previously they were elected.

As suggested above, the position of U.S. presidents is less ambiguous:

> I do not micro-manage but I appoint deans and provosts who act on my behalf. I oversee their work.

One UK vice chancellor discussed this issue with two American presidents. He said:

Amy Gutmann [president of the University of Pennsylvania] and Shirley Tilghman [president of Princeton] are amazed about the amount
of work that I have to get involved with where they can appoint line
managers or provosts.

As mentioned earlier, in European universities, power has often been allowed
to reside in committees. In the United Kingdom this is changing; indeed,
some leaders have apparently started to flex their muscles when it comes to
the old notion of collegiality:

> The committees do not take decisions—even if that is what they think
> they do. They merely endorse decisions. I have tried to weaken the
> committee structures or at least function outside of it. But I try to take
> the committees with me in terms of the decisions I want to make.

One UK head put his position on the line:

> I made it clear to Senate that has 60 members; they may have had
> access and input into planning and resources before, but not any more.
> Senate is to have no budgetary powers and if they were not willing to
> accept this then I was not willing to stay in the job . . . Collegiality
> doesn't mean everyone makes decisions.

The issues of strategy, power, and democracy are further discussed in chapters 5 and 6.

A SUMMARY OF WHAT IS COMING UP

This book has been written with world universities in mind. I believe these
findings are generalizable across borders. Some of my data are international
in the broadest sense, although the interviews with university heads are from
the United States and the United Kingdom.

It is important that the conclusions rest on a disinterested reading of the
data gathered. As mentioned earlier, I draw from quantitative and qualitative
evidence. I have resisted putting the statistical information into an appendix;
instead, I have tried to present the findings in the text so that they are
accessible to nonstatisticians. Quantitative evidence is presented in chapters
2 to 4, but the qualitative data, consisting mostly of statements from leaders
in research universities, appears intermittently throughout the book. Many
of my central arguments have come directly from comments made in interviews. It is here, arguably, where objectivity is particularly difficult for an
outsider to check. In the interviews there is of course supposition, and the
explanations I present about *why* and *how* scholar-leaders might improve
their institutions are supported solely by interviews and argument. But my

hope is that an unconventional mixing of the qualitative and the quantitative provides some advantages.

There are approximately four hundred leaders in the quantitative dataset, plus thirty-two semistructured qualitative interviews. The data collection process is explained in appendix 1, where the names and positions of those interviewed are also listed. The research quality of presidents and vice chancellors is assessed in this book by using citations and bibliometric data. To compare across disciplines—for example, to contrast the lifetime citations of a biologist with an economist or historian—the different individuals' citations must be normalized. Appendix 2 has information about how the citations were collected, the normalization method, and general information on the use of bibliometric data.

Regarding the nomenclature of leaders' titles, I opt for simplicity rather than detailed precision. I will mostly refer to the executive heads (akin to CEOs in the for-profit sector) as university *presidents*, which will include labels such as vice chancellor, rector, principal, director, and so on.[36] In the next few sections, I summarize briefly what is coming up in the book.

I begin to analyze the quantitative evidence in chapter 2; specifically, I uncover who are the leaders of the world's top 100 universities. If the best institutions—that arguably have the widest choice of candidates—systematically appoint top scholars as their presidents, this could be one form of evidence that, on average, better researchers make better presidents. Economists would call this a revealed preference argument. Also in the next chapter, I offer descriptive information about the 100 global universities. Most notably, I find a positive correlation between the lifetime citations of a university's president and the position of that university in the global ranking. The higher the university is in the international league table, the higher the lifetime citations of its leader. I show that this pattern exists for my full global sample of 100 universities, and for the subsample of U.S. universities. However, when I isolate non-U.S. institutions the pattern largely disappears. In other words, American research universities appear to be selecting their leaders differently. This is interesting because the sample of U.S. institutions that I examine in this chapter include the world's very best. Scholars in the same group of universities are also winning the majority of Nobel Prizes. I present bar diagrams and a scatter plot showing that the number of Nobel laureates in European universities has declined strongly over the last fifty years; whereas Nobels being won by researchers in the top U.S. institutions has risen remarkably (further into appendix 4, I discuss the issue of why).

[36] The term *vice chancellor* (or VC) will be used in chapter 4 where the data include a sample only from the United Kingdom. The titles of *Chancellor* and *Vice Chancellor* are also used in public universities in the United States.

Chapter 3 looks for a similar pattern in a different dataset. Here I go inside universities and isolate a particular unit, the business school. The president may stop the buck, but there are many leaders in universities. I choose to look at business schools because they are often among the largest departments in universities, and business schools have the interesting but complicated task of reaching out to two communities—researchers and practitioners. Again, I look for a relationship between the citations, this time of deans, and the ranked position of a business school in the *Financial Times* global MBA ranking. Because of the dual function of schools of business and management, it might be expected that a significant relationship would not exist. Yet, again, using cross-sectional data, a positive correlation is found between the position of a business school in the ranking and the prior research achievement of its dean; better scholars appear also to be leading better business schools.

Chapter 4 attempts to go beyond cross-section patterns. Its aim is to address questions of causality. This is done by drawing upon longitudinal information. I look at the performance of a university, and then trace back to examine the characteristics of its leader a number of years earlier. Using an appropriate measure of performance, one that has existed in the United Kingdom since 1986—the so-called Research Assessment Exercise—I try to identify whether universities that performed well in the Research Assessment Exercise tended to be led by strong scholars. Here the data come from fifty-five UK research universities, namely, those institutions that competed in the RAE in 1992, 1996, and 2001. Using regression analysis, the study uncovers evidence that seems consistent with the existence of a causal relationship between the research ability of a leader and the *future* performance of his or her university.

Interview material appears throughout the book. However, chapter 5 draws exclusively from qualitative data. It presents arguments about how and why scholar-leaders improve the performance of their universities. I start the chapter by focusing on the unanswered questions that arise from the simple cross-section correlations; specifically, do richer or better universities hire more distinguished scholars merely because they can? This would suggest that any causality goes the other way. Or, perhaps the point is that good scholars are simply good at everything? I attempt to dispel these arguments, and then move on to the oft-debated topic of hiring nonacademics as heads of research universities. Overwhelmingly, those leaders that I interviewed are opposed to the selection of outsiders. One UK vice chancellor later equates the issue with heads in the British National Health Service (NHS); he suggests that many of the problems in the NHS have stemmed from the fact that managers, who are not health practitioners and researchers, have been put in charge.

It is important to point out that a leader should represent the aspirations of the institution. Hiring a Nobel Prize winner to head up a university starting at a low research base is unlikely to be successful. In this chapter I also suggest that because individuals tend to select others who are like themselves, it is imperative that good scholars are on hiring and tenure committees. Finally, I turn attention to the ways that outstanding researchers can make an impact, including the many positive spillover effects both in a region and a university. I close by briefly arguing that having distinguished scholars at the helm of research universities is not sufficient; scholar-leaders should also lead organizations, like government funding bodies, that support universities.

Chapter 6 looks at how leaders get selected. A president interviewed in this book remarked that universities often rotate between hiring a strong scholar and then, as their successor, a weaker one. Thus I have asked the question: is there evidence that leaders may be chosen partially because they differ markedly from their predecessors—creating a kind of alternating leader cycle? If evidence of such a pendulum effect is found, it raises questions about how this form of selection might affect, adversely or otherwise, institutional strategy and organizational performance. For example, how much does an alteration in leader create a change in the direction of an organization? In a dataset of 157 leaders in fifty-five research universities, I observe two successive changes of leader per institution. The findings presented in bar diagrams and statistically suggest, quite strongly, that an alternating leader cycle does exist. Therefore, it could be argued that higher-education governing bodies appear to be selecting leaders in part because they differ from those they follow into the top job. The implications of this are discussed. I then present evidence from a case study where members of a university leader's hiring committee are interviewed. Although the findings are limited, because this is a look at only a single university, they may help to throw open the lid on a fascinating procedure that is rarely written about. It focuses attention on how leaders are chosen: is the process strategic or arbitrary? In other words, are university heads chosen because they fit the requirements of a long-term strategy? I also refer to comments, from presidents and vice chancellors interviewed for the book, about their own selection processes; and I uncover the doubts that exist about the quality of knowledge among many on university boards. This prompts a discussion in the book about governors and the involvement of boards in designing long-term strategies for universities.

In chapter 7, I move outside universities. I look at some other types of knowledge-based organizations where expert leadership is appropriate. The first arena I explore is a sports one—basketball. I report on coauthored work where it is shown that basketball coaches who were better players a number of years earlier accrue the highest number of wins as team heads. The "expert knowledge" effect of having been a top basketball player appears to be large, and, significantly, to be visible in the data within the first year of a new coach arriving. I suggest that expert knowledge may allow coaches who were better players to devise winning strategies since they may be able to "see" the game in ways that others cannot. Elsewhere in the book I suggest that professional service firms, such as accounting, consulting, or architecture practices, are fairly similar to universities. Their main business is in offering expert knowledge. Interview statements from a small number of heads of such firms (listed in appendix 1) reveal that the worlds of professionals seem similar to faculty in universities; in particular, leaders, often senior partners, must first be credible experts. Unlike what happens occasionally in universities, a firm's head is not likely to be someone from outside of the profession. Interesting comments are made from interviewees about how one identifies future senior partners, the necessary training and the challenges of maintaining one's expert credibility while leading a practice or firm. Finally in chapter 7, I look briefly toward the arts and ponder whether the great leadership successes of a conductor might partially be attributable to his artistic ability.

In chapter 8, I conclude. A paradox has existed in leadership research. Its intellectual status within business schools has been low, yet demand from MBA students, among others, is high. This study attempts to use objective measures to analyze leadership and performance in a particular form of knowledge-intensive organization—research universities. The book ends by suggesting the kinds of reader that I hope might be interested in this work.

CHAPTER TWO

LEADERS OF THE WORLD'S
TOP UNIVERSITIES

THE MOST PRESTIGIOUS AND WEALTHIEST universities arguably have the widest choice of leadership candidates. If it can be shown that they appoint top scholars as their leaders, this could be one form of evidence that, on average, better researchers may make better university presidents.[1] Economists would call this a form of "revealed preference" (about the organizations' underlying objectives). As suggested earlier, scholarship is not viewed here as a proxy for either management experience or leadership skills but something *in addition* to that. However, a priori, if what really matters in a leader is managerial ability, it would not be expected that universities would be led by successful researchers.

In this chapter[2] I use statistical tests to identify whether the world's top universities currently appoint top scholars to the position of president. When looking at the individuals who run these great institutions, it is possible to find both a handful of heavily cited scholars and a handful of leaders with few or no research citations. It might be thought from this fact that there is no systematic link between research output and university leadership. Yet, as I will show, there is a pattern. A significant correlation exists between the research background of a leader and the position of their university in a world league table.

As discussed in chapter 1, institutional heads probably hold the most influential positions of authority in a university. But there are other strategic leadership positions that are only a step down from presidents, for example, deans of schools. In chapter 3 I turn to one such group—business school deans.

In the quantitative analyses in the next three chapters, I focus on one set of measures of a university leader's research performance, namely, the person's lifetime scholarly citations. Citations are references to authors in other academic papers as acknowledgment of their contribution to a specific research area. The process of building academic knowledge is done partly by referencing important work that has gone before. That referencing—the citing of

---

[1] The term *president* will be used again to represent all university heads—vice chancellors, rectors, directors, principals, among other titles.

[2] This chapter draws upon Goodall (2006b).

those earlier contributions—is the cornerstone of academic research. Citations are generally viewed as a reliable indicator of research achievement over time. I gathered the bibliometric information by hand counting the lifetime citations of each leader in my dataset—just over four hundred individuals. Hand counting is necessary because an electronic count creates so many errors due to homonyms and other problems (see appendix 1 for information on the data collection process).

Publishing conventions differ across academic disciplines. For example, scientists publish many more articles than social scientists, and subsequently they tend to accrue higher numbers of citations, while far fewer are assigned in the humanities. To adjust for this discrepancy, each leader's lifetime citations are later normalized into what I call a citations "P-score" = president's individual lifetime citations normalized for discipline. I will use a president's normalized citation score—or P-score—in chapters 2 and 4. (Information about citations and the normalization process is presented in appendix 2.)

Why use citations instead of journal articles? There is a growing body of work that uses citations, often with other measures, to assess intellectual output and productivity. Importantly, citations tend to signify research quality, insofar as other authors recognize the work. Moreover, citation counts are a good predictor of both professorial salaries and Nobel Prizes. An alternative approach is to count an author's published articles and weight by journal impact factors. However, this presents three problems. First, books and monographs would be completely excluded from the data. Second, the quality of a journal is a noisy measure of the future impact of individual articles. For example, many highly cited articles are not published in Grade A journals and vice versa. Finally, assigning weight to journal quality through, for example, ISI Journal Impact Factors might not be reliable—even if they were available—for papers published ten to twenty years ago. Also, impact factors still rely on citations data.[3]

Thus, citation scores are used here as a measure of how research-active and successful a president has been in his or her academic career. Most academics who go into administrative positions reduce their research output. This depends, somewhat, on their discipline. The data generated in this study make it clear that university presidents accumulate the overwhelming majority (approximately 90 to 95 percent) of their citations before they become institutional leaders.

The emphasis in this chapter and the next is on leaders of the world's top research universities and business schools, because it is both interesting and important to understand the actions of successful organizations.

---

[3] See Hamermesh, Johnson, and Weisbrod (1982) for salaries; Garfield and Welljams-Dorof (1992) for Nobels; and Oswald (2006) for journal quality versus article impact. For discussion about journal impact factors see Moed (2002).

THE TOP 100 UNIVERSITIES

Identifying whether better universities select reputable scholars as presidents tells us something about the actions of top institutions, and also gives us a starting place for trying to understand whether universities might actually perform better under their leadership. If there is no association between the characteristic of scholarship and university quality, then my hypothesis that research universities achieve more when led by distinguished scholars is unlikely to be correct.

To discover which universities occupy the top positions requires the use of rankings. League tables are ubiquitous and have a long history. Reputational rankings were used in the United States at the turn of the nineteenth century. Clark Kerr, chancellor of Berkeley in the 1950s, talks in his book *The Gold and the Blue*[4] of how he and others at Berkeley used rankings to motivate change and improve the university. Kerr's yearning was to overtake Harvard, Yale, Princeton, and other top U.S. institutions—a desire that was eventually met in 1964, when the American Council of Education placed Berkeley at number one.[5]

As higher education has become global, in the recruitment of international students and staff, so have rankings. International tables have existed for a number of years in areas such as business education through the *Financial Times*. In 2003 the first global league table of universities was produced by the Institute of Education in Shanghai at Jiao Tong University (SJTU). Jiao Tong scholars generated the table to help them assess how Chinese universities compare with those in different nations.

To identify the top 100 universities in the world, I use the "Academic Ranking of World Universities" 2004 (the full list of institutions is available in appendix 3). Another global table was created in 2004; one produced by the British-based *Times Higher Education*.[6] I chose the Jiao Tong table because it uses a more rigorous method of assessment, and it is not produced by a commercial publication.[7] Media-generated league tables are controversial.

[4] Kerr (2001).
[5] An Assessment of Quality in Graduate Education (1966), by the American Council of Education, Washington DC.
[6] See www.timeshighereducation.co.uk. *Times Higher Education* (THE) was formerly known as *Times Higher Education Supplement* (THES).
[7] The main problem with the THE league table is that 50 percent weight is assigned to a subjective "peer-review" process where 1,300 academics across eighty-eight countries are invited to name the top institutions in their geographic area and their academic field. This is the largest component in the ranking, yet there is no information available on the background of these scholars. This is a concern. For example, how might an individual's choice have been influenced by their own place of education, sabbatical leave, or coauthorship, and so on?

Rankings, such as those in *U.S. News and World Report* in North America and the *Guardian* newspaper in the United Kingdom, offer information to potential students across a range of criteria. They may be useful heuristic devices for students but as objective tools of assessment of university quality they are often unreliable. Perhaps the main criticism is that, because they are produced by for-profit organizations that want to sell their publications, a headline is required. To generate a story, the methodology is changed, sometimes annually, which ensures that institutions at the top rotate. In the United States, university positions actually change very little each year if a fixed method of analysis is used.[8]

The "Academic Ranking of World Universities" (2004) league table uses six different criteria to assess university quality.[9] There are, arguably, some weaknesses in the Jiao Tong methodology. First, younger universities stand to lose out, particularly in the first category that assigns weight (10 percent) to alumni awards. On the one hand, many universities are simply too new to have generated substantial numbers of alumni winning awards such as Nobel Prizes. Institutions like Oxford, on the other hand, can more easily trade off their past success. Second, the humanities and the social sciences are weakly represented—though the Jiao Tong researchers have made a number of adjustments since 2004.[10] The Awards category is also limited. Nobel Prizes are only given for achievement in physics, chemistry, medicine/physiology, economics, literature, and peace, and Fields Medals only for mathematics.

An important factor in using the Jiao Tong table is that their ranking compares favorably with other noncommercial league tables. Therefore, we can expect to find the same institutions ranked in approximately the same positions in other tables.[11]

In the next few sections I present information about the 100 universities and their leaders.

WHERE ARE THE TOP UNIVERSITIES LOCATED?

The top research universities in the world are overwhelmingly located in the United States. In the top 100 table, 51 institutions are to be found there. As can be seen in figure 2.1, U.S. institutions are unevenly spread across the 100. They dominate the top end of the league table. Seventeen universities in the top 20 group are American, with 30 appearing among the top 40 in the world. Of the 100 total, only 4 in the bottom quintile are U.S. based.

[8] Lombardi et al. (2002, 2003).
[9] See appendix 3.
[10] For details, go to their Web site at www.ed.sjtu.edu.cn/ranking.
[11] See for example the ranking in Lombardi et al. (2003).

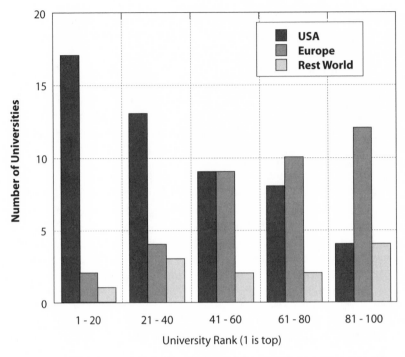

Figure 2-1. The cross-country distribution of the world's top 100 universities

That so many outstanding universities are located in the United States is notable if not surprising (given its wealth and large population). The United States attracts the highest number of international academics of any nation, focusing specifically on the very best. In the top ten departments of economics, 75 percent of assistant professors did their first degree outside the United States, signifying that it is unlikely they are American by birth.[12]

Nobel Prizes are far more likely to be awarded to scholars in the United States. In the field of physics, a UK-based scholar has not won a Nobel since the 1970s. Figure 2.2 shows the percentage of Nobel Prizes awarded to individuals based in universities in eight European countries—Austria, France, Germany, Italy, Netherlands, Sweden, Switzerland, and the United Kingdom—between 1900 and 1950. These nations are the largest recipients of Nobel Prizes after the United States. As can be seen, the proportion of prizes acquired by these nations up to the 1950s outweighed those awarded to U.S.-located scholars. Prizes include only those given for chemistry, medicine, physics, and later in economics. (The Nobel Prize in econom-

---

[12] A recent paper that looks at the international brain drain is produced by the University of Warwick (2007).

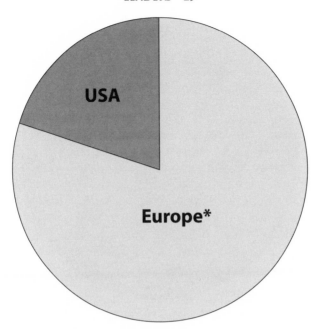

Figure 2-2. Share of Nobel Prizes awarded to individuals in institutions in Europe and the USA 1900–1950

* European countries are: Austria, France, Germany, Italy, Netherlands, Sweden, Switzerland, and the UK. Data from www.nobleprize.org.

ics was introduced in 1969.) I have focused, in figure 2.2, on the location of the university with which a Nobel laureate is associated, and not a laureate's birth nation. Arguably, the positive influence, or spillover effects, of a prize winner is more likely to benefit the institution or country where he or she is living.

Figure 2.3 then depicts the number of Nobel Prizes awarded in Europe and the United States after 1950. This shows that there is a decline among European nations as recipients.

Figure 2.4 presents the information differently, focusing specifically on the decline in France, Germany, and the United Kingdom as compared with the rise in Nobel laureates in the United States.[13] Switzerland is somewhat the exception among European countries, because it wins the highest pro-

[13] The number of scientific papers and citations accrued by UK scholars has kept pace, proportionally, with U.S. output. Charlton (2007a and 2007b) argues that the United Kingdom does badly in Nobel Prizes partially because it invests in what he considers to be the wrong type of science. He argues that the most ambitious science is intrinsically riskier, and therefore more likely to fail. Whereas in the United Kingdom, he suggests, many of the best scientists seek to extend knowledge more modestly and to build incrementally on

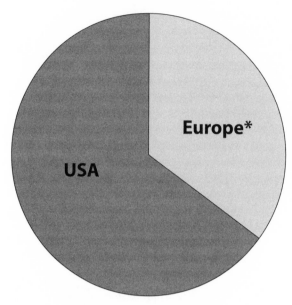

Figure 2-3. Share of Nobel Prizes awarded to individuals in institutions in Europe and the USA 1951–2007

* European countries are: Austria, France, Germany, Italy, Netherlands, Sweden, Switzerland, and the UK. Data from www.nobleprize.org.

portion of Nobel Prizes per head of population in the world.[14] (For discussion about whether it matters that Europe's Nobel's are declining please see appendix 4.)

If I treat American states as individual nations, California, with a population of 36 million, has the highest number of leading universities. Ten California institutions are ranked within the top 55. Six of these are among the top 20, and 7 of the 10 are public or state universities.

There are 37 institutions out of the 100 located in European countries. The largest European group, 11, is in the United Kingdom. British universities perform relatively well in the SJTU table. Seven of the top 100 are in Germany. German research universities once provided the model for many of the top U.S. institutions, though arguably they have slipped somewhat since their heyday.[15] The first German institution to appear in the

---

existing ideas and methods. The United Kingdom's funding mechanisms and the Research Assessment Exercise that reports on average every five years, may accentuate this.

[14] Switzerland wins 0.5 Nobel Prizes per 1 million population (information available from Institut der deutschen Wirtschaft Köln).

[15] The quality of German universities was perceived to have declined by the German government, so in 2006 it announced that three universities would be given elite status

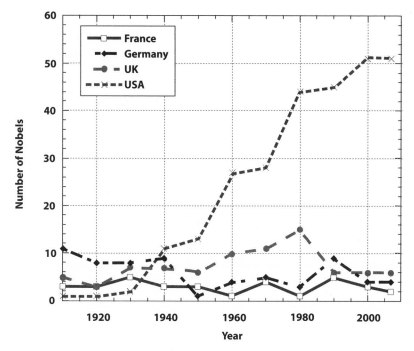

Figure 2-4. Number of Nobel Prizes awarded to individuals in institutions in France, Germany, United Kingdom, and USA between 1900 and 2007

100 table in 2004 is the Technical University of Munich, ranked 45th. Notably, it is led by the most cited of all the presidents of German universities in the sample.

In the top 100, there are 4 universities based in France, which is another nation previously envied for its higher education.[16] The first appears at position 41 in the league table. In Sweden, a country with a population of only 9 million, there are 4 universities among the group. Three of the 37 European institutions are located in Switzerland. With just 7.5 million people, Switzerland is second only after the United States in attracting highly cited scientists to its universities academic faculties.[17] There are 2 universities in the Nether-

receiving extra government funding. Karlsruhe, the University of Munich, and the Technical University of Munich were the universities chosen.

[16] In 2007 President Nicolas Sarkozy announced that he would introduce legislation to reform France's universities, because they compared badly in the SJTU and other league tables with universities in the United States and to a lesser degree the United Kingdom.

[17] The numbers are small compared with the United States. See the paper by the University of Warwick (2007). In 1998 the voters of the Canton of Zurich approved a new University Law that gave Zurich University the status of an autonomous legal entity. Many at the University of Zurich believe this has led to raised standards.

lands—both led by highly cited presidents; and 1 each located in Austria, Denmark, Finland, Norway, Italy, and Russia.

Finally, among the top 100 there are 12 universities in the rest of the world—5 located in Japan, with Tokyo University highly ranked in position 14 in the world. There are 4 universities in Canada. Toronto is ranked highest at 24. Australia has 2 universities among the worlds' leading 100, and finally there is one Israeli institution, Hebrew University in Jerusalem, which is ranked 90th.

The location of a university is not always mirrored by the nationality of its president. For example, the top 10 universities are found in two countries, the United States (8) and United Kingdom (2), whereas their leaders come from four: Canada, New Zealand, United Kingdom, and the United States.

WHO ARE THE TOP 100 UNIVERSITIES' PRESIDENTS?

There are fifteen female presidents in the sample. Interestingly, six are in the top 20 group: at Cambridge, MIT, Princeton, UC San Diego, University of Pennsylvania, and University of Michigan.[18] This shows that women have been selected as leaders into some of the best universities in the world. North America dominates, with nine female presidents in the United States, and two in Canada. The remaining four are in Denmark, France, Sweden, and the United Kingdom. The disciplinary breakdown of the fifteen women is seven scientists, seven social scientists, and one from the humanities. One president, from the University of California, San Diego, is highly cited (listed in ISI HiCi—see below).

Every president in the group of 100 universities has a PhD. The majority have been academics, although two presidents spent most of their careers in industry or government, and a small group went almost directly into academic administration. It might not have been predicted that 100 percent of the presidents would have PhDs, or that 98 of the top 100 universities in the world appointed a scholar to the top job. This seems interesting in relation to the central argument in this book.

The mean age of the one hundred presidents is fifty-nine years. The age of leaders may potentially affect their lifetime citation score, because those who are older have had the greatest opportunity to accrue citations. Hence, for example, if the presidents with low numbers of citations can be shown to be significantly younger than those with high lifetime scores, age could be influential. However, inspection of the age profile of all leaders in my

[18] Harvard hired Drew Faust as president following Lawrence Summers, and the University of Wisconsin at Madison has recently appointed Biddy Martin as chancellor. Thus, it appears the trend is continuing.

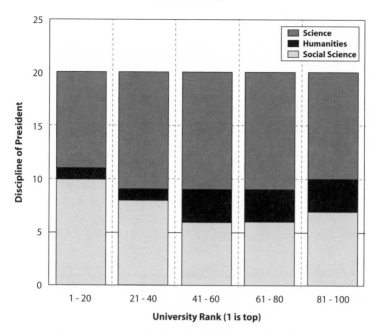

Figure 2-5. The disciplines of the presidents of the world's top universities

dataset finds that there are not significant age differences between those with the highest and lowest citation scores. Therefore, age cannot be said to have any major effect.[19] (This is discussed further in appendix 2.)

Figure 2.5 displays the disciplinary backgrounds of the university heads— for example, whether they were formerly scientists or faculty from the humanities. What is noticeable is the consistency of spread across each quintile. Of the one hundred presidents, fifty-two have a scientific background. The scientists are dominated by the life sciences at 50 percent, but there are also eleven engineers, six physicists, five chemists, and four computer scientists.

Thirty-seven of the one hundred presidents are social scientists. The largest disciplinary group among the social scientists is that of lawyers, who number fifteen. Within a second group of sixteen there is an even spread of educationalists, political scientists, sociologists, and those from public and social policy. Finally, there are six economists.

Eleven presidents are from the arts and humanities. This group has become noticeably smaller. In the 1930s, universities were led predominantly

[19] For interesting work on "The Life Cycles of Nobel Laureates in Economics" see Galenson and Weinberg (2005). The same authors also look at age and the quality of work produced by artists (2000).

TABLE **2.1**
Distribution of 100 Presidents' Lifetime Citations

	Unadjusted Citations	Normalized P-scores	P-scores of Top 50 Leaders	P-scores of Next 50 Leaders
Mean	2,731	6.03	8.76	3.30
Median	371	2.27	4.57	0.93

by scholars from the humanities.[20] That increasing numbers of leaders are scientists seems an indication of the prominence of science and technology in today's research establishments. Government funding in most countries is skewed toward scientific research.[21] Yet student demand for social science subjects, such as economics and business studies, has tended to outstrip demand for degrees in, say, languages. Thus institutional heads reflect these changes.

THE DISTRIBUTION OF CITATIONS

Information on the distribution of the one hundred presidents normalized lifetime citations, or P-scores, is shown in table 2.1. Of the one hundred presidents in this sample, twelve are outstanding researchers. They are listed as among the most highly cited in their field. Thomson Publishing has created a highly cited (ISI HiCi) category that identifies approximately the top 250 academic researchers (depending somewhat on discipline) across twenty-one broad subject areas.[22] However, at the time of writing, no HiCi's are yet assigned by ISI for subjects in the arts or humanities.

Highly cited leaders are more common in the top universities. Of the twelve presidents listed in ISI highlycited.com, six are running institutions in the top 20 group of universities: at Harvard, Stanford, Berkeley, California

[20] Breakwell and Tytherleigh (2007) show, in a dataset of UK vice chancellors from 1997 to 2006, that there has been an increase in the number of social scientists becoming leaders. Taylor (1986) documents the disciplinary distribution of vice chancellors and principals in the United Kingdom in an earlier period. He cites earlier work by Collison and Millen (1969) who showed that in the United Kingdom between 1935 and 1967 the proportion of heads from the arts declined from 68 percent to 48 percent while scientists rose from 19 percent to 41 percent. Taylor then reports his own findings, that by 1981, 67 percent of vice chancellors and principals were scientists, 13 percent were from the social sciences, and less than 20 percent were from the arts. Cohen and March (1974) showed a similar pattern in the number of U.S. presidents from the arts between 1924 and 1969.
[21] Data available from the Organisation for Economic Co-Operation and Development (OECD) at www.oecd.org.
[22] See www.isihighlycited.com.

Institute of Technology, UC San Diego, and UC San Francisco. There are three HiCi's among the next 20 universities, two in the next quintile, and one among the last group of twenty leaders. Finally, there are three Nobel Prize winners among the presidents (all in medicine)—two in the top 20 and one in the 20–40 category.

The distribution of citations across the one hundred presidents fits an application that is often used in bibliometric research, the phenomenon of Lotka's Law of scientific productivity.[23] Lotka describes the frequency of publication by academic authors. For example, of all authors in a specific field, say sociology, Lotka's law argues that approximately 60 percent will publish just one article, 15 percent will have two publications, and 7 percent of authors will publish three pieces, and so on. According to the law, only 6 percent of the authors in a given field will produce more than ten articles. Lotka notes an empirical regularity that the percentage or relative frequency of authors in a field who have published a certain number of articles appears to be inversely related to the square of the number of articles concerned.[24] This empirical regularity is, of course, most accurate when applied over long periods of time and to large bodies of work—for example, individuals' lifetime citations. A version of this law using presidents' citations applies here and is presented in figure 2.6.

ARE LEADERS IN THE TOP UNIVERSITIES MORE HIGHLY CITED?

If we look at the evidence presented in this section, the answer is yes. They are more highly cited. A simple representation of the results can be seen in figure 2.7. The bar diagram shows the average P-scores (lifetime citations normalized for discipline) of each president by the position each university is ranked in the Jiao Tong global league table. Here I have grouped the 100 universities into quintiles (the 1–20 group always refers to the top of the SJTU table and 1 equals Harvard).

Figure 2.7 confirms that highly ranked universities have leaders who are more highly cited. Indeed, there is a clear monotonic decline in presidents' citation levels as the universities go down in world rank. Those leading the top 50 universities are approximately two and a half times more highly cited

---

[23] Lotka (1926), Potter (1988). Thanks for suggestions from G. D. A. Brown and Mark Taylor.

[24] The number making n contributions is about $1/n^2$ of those making one ($Y = K/X^2$, where X is the number of publications, Y the relative frequency of authors with X publications, and K is a constant). The fact that the presidents' citations data obeys this known empirical regularity suggests that the data are not abnormal and that inferences drawn upon them are likely to be valid.

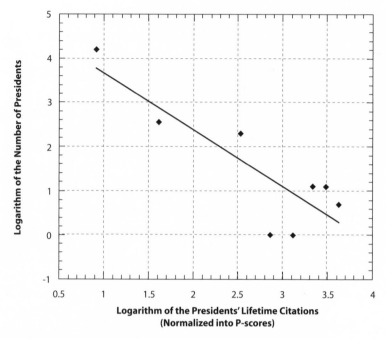

Figure 2-6. The distribution of presidents' lifetime citations follows Lotka's Law of Scientific Productivity

than those in the bottom 50. A president in a top 20 university typically has five times the lifetime citations of a leader in the bottom quintile.

The next step is to see if the relationship is statistically significant.[25] In other words, can we be sure that the correlation between a president's research success and the rank position of their university is robust? Using Pearson's correlation coefficient (r), the degree of linear relationship between the "rank of university" and "president's P-score" can be examined. Figure 2.8 shows the statistical finding in the form of a scatter plot. The results are also presented in table 2.2, and I have included four different subsamples:

(1) The group of one hundred presidents,
(2) a subset of fifteen female university presidents,

[25] A natural first approach is to test whether the rank ordering of one variable is correlated with the rank order of the second variable. Spearman's rank correlation coefficient is an appropriate measure. The highest P-score is ranked 1 and the lowest P-score is ranked 100. The actual rank of presidents' P-scores is then tested for a correlation against university rank. Using these data, Spearman's rho is calculated at 0.378. With 100 observations the associated 5 percent critical value for a two-tailed test is 0.195, and at 1 percent it is 0.254, which establishes that the correlation is statistically significant at conventional confidence levels.

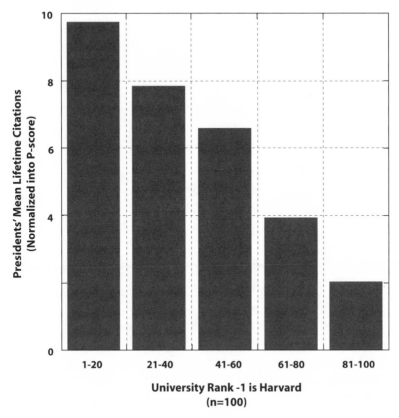

Figure 2-7. Presidents who lead universities higher in a world university ranking have higher lifetime citations (in quintiles)

(3) presidents from the United States only, who number fifty-one, and finally,

(4) presidents leading universities in the rest of the world, who number forty-nine.

The one hundred presidents are examined first. Column (1) in table 2.2 gives the result for the distribution of the one hundred individual presidents' P-scores by world university rank. As can be seen, the level of statistical significance indicates that a strong correlation exists between a leader's citations and the rank position of their university.[26] The analysis confirms the simple cross-sectional bar diagram in figure 2.7 above: as universities ascend the Jiao Tong league table, so does the level of scholarship of the university's president.

[26] There continues to be a statistically significant relationship if the natural logarithm of P-score is used ($p < 0.01$).

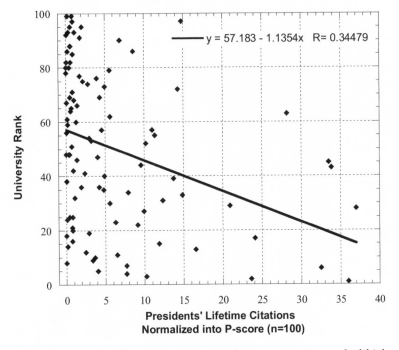

Figure 2-8. Presidents' lifetime citations are higher in universities ranked higher in a global league table

It is interesting to see if the relationship between presidents' citations and university quality exists within the group of women presidents (although at fifteen the sample is necessarily small). The result in column (2) in table 2.2 shows that, again, the variables are positively correlated. That the correlation is still robust even among a small subsample seems to be notable. To see the pattern in the distribution of the fifteen women presidents, I have represented the findings in a scatter plot in figure 2.9. The position of a university in the Shanghai table (dependent variable) is on the Y axis with the women's citation levels (independent variable) on the X axis.

Does the Same Pattern Exist among the Group of U.S. Presidents?

Of those in the world's top 100 ranking, 51 of the universities are located in the United States. Of the twelve highly cited[27] presidents in the one hun-

---

[27] Those, loosely, in the top 250 in their academic discipline.

TABLE **2.2**
Results of Cross-sectional Correlations of Presidents' P-scores by
University Rank from Four Different Sub-Samples

Pearson's Correlation Coefficient between Lifetime Citations and Rank	(1) Presidents of Top 100 Universities (n = 100)	(2) Female Presidents (n = 15)	(3) U.S. Presidents (n = 51)	(4) Presidents from the Rest of the World (n = 49)
	0.344***	0.690**	0.375**	0.140

***p < 0.001;   **p < 0.01

dred total, nine are based in U.S. universities, although two of these are non-Americans. One of them is from Canada, and one from the United Kingdom, who is also a Nobel Prize winner. The data show that there is a difference in the research backgrounds of presidents in the United States compared with the non-American leaders. The mean P-score (normalized lifetime citations) for the U.S. group of presidents is 8.07 with a median score of 4.86. These scores are higher than the averages for the total one hundred presidents. The mean P-score for the whole group is 6.03, and median P-score is 2.27. Therefore, on average, American universities seem to be appointing more accomplished scholars.

The bar diagram in Figure 2.10 presents the fifty-one U.S. presidents by the position of their university in the global ranking separated into quartiles. The pattern reveals a clear correlation. As can be seen, those leading the top quarter of U.S. universities have higher levels of lifetime citations than those in the lowest quartile. Again the pattern shows a monotonic decline in the position of a university and its president's citation levels. If we then check the findings statistically, we can see in table 2.2 in column (3) that, once again, the relationship is significant.

It could be argued that U.S. presidents have a higher number of citations merely because of publishing bias. For example, the majority of academic journals listed in ISI Web of Knowledge are U.S.-based, so editors and researchers may discriminate in favor of their own. Some international ones, especially in foreign languages, are excluded. However, four of the most highly cited presidents in the one hundred sample have come from universities outside the United States (United Kingdom, Germany, and two from the Netherlands). For the purposes of this research, by focusing solely on the U.S. presidents, I am creating a control group in which these potential biases are diminished.

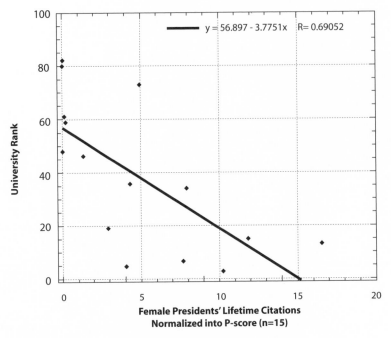

Figure 2-9. Female presidents' lifetime citations are higher in universities ranked higher in a global league table

Is the Citation-Rank Correlation True for Universities outside the United States?

So far I have identified a strong positive relationship between the citation levels of university presidents and the position of their institution within a ranking of 100 universities. This association exists among the one hundred presidents in total, the group of fifteen women leaders, and the fifty-one U.S. presidents. However, as we shall see, this pattern does not exist for the remaining group of universities in other countries.

In the group of non-U.S. institutions I find that the statistical relationship is no longer robust. To remind ourselves of where the 49 institutions in the rest of the world are located, there are: 37 universities in Europe (11 are in the United Kingdom, 7 in Germany, 4 in both France and Sweden, 3 in Switzerland, 2 in the Netherlands, and 1 each in Austria, Denmark, Finland, Norway, Italy, and Russia). Five universities are based in Japan, 4 are in Canada, 2 in Australia, and 1 in Israel.

Presidents in universities in the rest of the world appear to have less-established research backgrounds when compared with U.S. leaders, who have significantly higher levels of lifetime citations. The mean citation P-

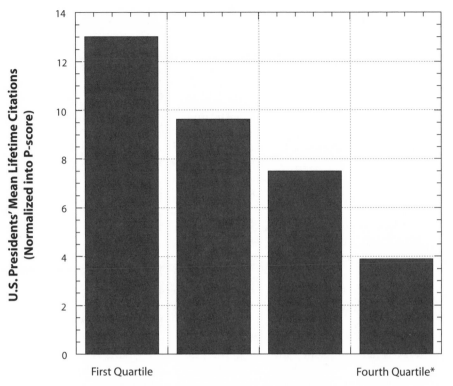

U.S. Universities Rank Position in Global Table Presented in Quartiles
(n=51)

Figure 2-10. U.S. presidents' lifetime citations are higher in universities ranked higher in the global league table (in quartiles)

score (normalized for discipline) for presidents located in the forty-nine non-U.S. countries is 3.91 with a median score of 1.07. This is below the 100-group mean P-score of 6.0 and is half the U.S. mean P-score of 8.0 (see table 2.1 above). Therefore U.S. presidents are twice as cited as those in the rest of the world.

The figures may be picking up bias in publishing: many of these leaders are from non-English-speaking nations. However, as has been suggested earlier, plenty of top scholars are leading non-U.S. institutions. Indeed, there are three highly cited leaders in this group. Two are based in the Netherlands, and one is in Germany.[28] It is unlikely, therefore, that the lower citation

---

[28] The fourth non-U.S. HiCi/Nobel is Paul Nurse who spent his career in the United Kingdom but moved to the United States to lead Rockefeller University in 2003.

levels across the forty-nine leaders in the non-U.S. nations can be explained entirely by language bias.

The figures in column (4) in table 2.2 confirm that there is no statistically significant correlation, between citation levels and position of president, across the forty-nine nations in the rest of the world.

An interesting final test is to focus on one of the countries among the forty-nine non-U.S. nations to see if a relationship can be found. The United Kingdom, with 11 institutions, has the highest number of universities in the top 100 after America. The mean lifetime citation P-score of the eleven UK presidents is 2.36, which is lower than the average P-score of presidents in the full group of forty-nine non-U.S. nations, at 3.91. This again demonstrates that the large discrepancy in the average citation scores of U.S. presidents when compared to those in the rest of the world is unlikely to be explained by English language bias. If it were, I would expect the P-scores of British heads to be higher than non-English speakers. With just eleven observations statistical inference should, of course, be viewed with caution. Nevertheless the scatter plot in figure 2.11 reveals that a modest relationship exists between the lifetime citation of UK university heads and the position of their institution in the global ranking. Thus it appears that the United Kingdom mimics, somewhat, hiring practices of the United States, although the scholarly standard—as measured by citations—of heads in British universities in this sample is lower than their U.S. counterparts.

In general, the evidence presented in this section demonstrates that presidential selection committees in universities outside of the United States appear to make different decisions about who should lead their institutions.

Are the figures influenced by outliers? The data presented above show quite convincingly that better universities select, on average, better researchers to run them. But are the results unduly influenced by a small number of presidents with extremely distinguished research backgrounds? To guard against this, I have performed a number of checks and the results remain robust.[29]

Is it a coincidence that the United States is home to many of the world's top research universities, while also having a higher number of proficient scholars in leadership positions? Data on world university rankings have only recently become available. The fact that universities with strongly research-intensive missions appoint as their presidents men and women with a high

---

[29] First, we can return to Spearman's rho, which puts an equal weight on each observation instead of assigning continuous values. As has been pointed out above, a statistically significant rank correlation has been established, with a significance level better than 1 percent. The second check on outliers is simply to delete the data used from the highest P-scores for the Pearson's test. To do this, the top 5 percent of P-scores, all located within ranges 30 and 40, were withdrawn and the correlation retested, with a result of 0.297. With ninety-five observations, the 1 percent critical value for a two-tailed test is 0.260, so the correlation remains.

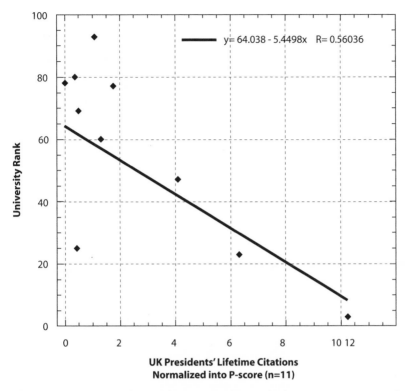

Figure 2-11. UK presidents' lifetime citations are higher in universities ranked higher in a global league table

number of citations does not appear to have been previously documented in the research literature. It is, needless to say, simply a fact—a pattern found in the data. The evidence I have presented does not enable judgments to be made about the weight assigned by selection committees to the research records of presidential candidates as distinct, for example, from other criteria such as managerial expertise or entrepreneurship. But one might believe that research universities look for candidates who fit institutional missions.

These findings show that, in at least one area, the leading universities are making different choices from those lower in the global ranking. On average, the higher the university is in the Jiao Tong league table, the more highly cited is that institution's president. There are, of course, exceptions. Two universities from the Netherlands—in positions 39 and 63—both have presidents who are classed by ISI Web of Knowledge as highly cited. (It is interesting to note that these are the only two universities in the top 100 from that country.) And there are top universities led by presidents with few or no citations. However, these cases are in a minority.

Universities perform a central role in society and the global economy. This is particularly true of the prominent research institutions that top most league tables. That these universities appoint better researchers to lead them seems an important finding.

An interesting next step might be to investigate whether a similar pattern exists in a substantial unit within a university, for example, a business school. This is done in the next chapter. But before moving on, it is interesting first to ponder why this pattern—the correlation between top-university ranking and scholar-leaders—has not been noted in the literature on leadership or universities.

Part of the reason for the gap may be a lack of hard data in leadership research. Books about leadership are often anecdotal. Moreover, the kind of pattern identified here might be difficult to pick up after a small number of meetings with university presidents, or through qualitative analysis. The correlation between smoking and cancer took many years to identify—the search for a causal relationship is still going on.

CONCLUDING COMMENTS

Universities high up in global league tables behave differently from the institutions lower down. They select leaders who are more highly cited. Because these top institutions have a wider pool of candidates from which to choose, this fact is interesting. Top institutions have cash and cachet. If Yale wanted a CEO from industry, they could presumably appoint one. Yet the top research universities appear to select, on average, accomplished scholars rather than professional managers.

Cross-sectional analysis can be suggestive of causality but, of course, is not sufficient to establish a causal relationship. However, the correlations presented here have been replicated a number of times in different subsamples. Among the 100 top universities in the world, there is a monotonic decline in the number of lifetime citations accrued by a president and the position of his or her institution in a global league table. For the group of 100 universities, on average I find that one extra point on a president's adjusted citation score (where scores run from zero for the least-cited president to a score of just under 40 for highly cited and Nobel Prize–winning presidents) is associated with ten extra places up the world's top 100 ranking of universities. A similar result is found in a subsample of fifteen women presidents. Again, a statistically significant correlation is identified between the ranked position of universities and the research histories of the women leading them. There is a strong relationship between the citations of American leaders and the global ranking of their institutions. An association exists among the subsample of 11 UK universities, although the lifetime citations of UK heads are markedly lower than their U.S. counterparts. But when the group of 49 universities from the rest of the world is examined together, no relationship exists, which suggests that U.S. universities are making different choices about whom they select as leader.

The next chapter looks at whether the same pattern exists among deans of the world's top 100 business schools. Then in chapter 4 I attempt to go beyond cross-section correlations and look at whether having better scholars at the helm actually improves future performance.

CHAPTER THREE

DEANS OF THE TOP BUSINESS SCHOOLS

UNIVERSITIES ARE MADE UP OF COLLECTIONS OF UNITS, such as faculties, schools, academic departments, and others. They differ in size and focus, and importantly they have their own leadership. It was shown in the last chapter that on average the world's top universities appoint more highly cited scholars to lead them. In this chapter, I examine whether a similar pattern exists in a particular unit within universities—namely business schools. I ask: are better business schools also being led by better scholars?

Schools of medicine, law, education, and business are, arguably, more complex than traditional academic departments, because they straddle the two communities of research and practice. Thus they are an interesting case. The question of how much it matters if a leader has been a scholar is one that has been much debated in business schools since their inception. Indeed nonacademics are more often selected to head business schools than to run universities—as we will later see.

This chapter presents a second empirical contribution, again a correlation.[1] It shows that the business schools that stand higher in the *Financial Times* global MBA ranking have deans with systematically higher levels of lifetime citations. This is for a sample of 100 business schools across nations. The robustness of the result is reinforced by the fact that I then find the same pattern, using a different performance measure in another dataset, among a set of UK business and management schools.

One reason business schools are interesting is that it is quite usual to find they are the largest single social-science department in a university. Not only has demand for management education spiraled over the last twenty years, but also business schools have often been viewed as earnings-cows by the universities that house them.[2] The Master of Business Administration (MBA) is routinely the most highly priced course offered in universities. Thus, it is natural to see whether business schools mimic universities by appointing leaders who have been successful scholars.

Another issue is relevant. Discussion about the applicability of management research has rumbled on for a number of years. Within the field, publishing output is expected to be both scholarly and relevant to the "real

---

[1] This work first appeared in a conference paper in 2006 (see Goodall [2006a]).
[2] Figures available at http://rankings.ft.com/businessschoolrankings/global-mba-rankings on number of MBAs.

world" of business. The potential conflict has generated considerable debate, and it continues.[3] A statement from a former business school dean interviewed for this book encapsulates this:

> The primary business of a business school is the same as a university—teaching and research, and administration. But with a business school there are another two objectives. First, to have credibility with the profession and have a high external profile amongst the business world, and second, to facilitate a twin-track of publishing—academic journals and also applied publications.

Because of the more complex brief of business schools in comparison to universities, one might not expect to find a relationship between the level of scholarship of a dean and the position of his or her school in the *FT* MBA ranking. But, again, there is a correlation. Business schools at the top end of the table select leaders who are more established researchers.

FINANCIAL TIMES GLOBAL MBA RANKING

As suggested in the previous chapter, media-generated league tables may offer students a snapshot of information, but as substantive assessments of quality they are untrustworthy. Rankings also typically exclude factors such as an institution's history, reputation, and wealth. However, it could be argued that because business schools are relatively new additions to the academy, and they are small in comparison with universities, there is a greater possibility of genuine movement within league tables or other performance measures.[4]

The *Financial Times* produces one of the more consistent league tables. It has the advantage that the methodology used for assessment remains largely unchanged each year. Another reason for selecting the *FT* league table is that it is internationally recognized. The *FT* ranking began as a European survey of 49 business schools in 1998 and developed into a worldwide league table of 75 schools in 2000. This number was extended to 100 in 2001. I am using the 2005 *Financial Times* MBA ranking in this study[5] (see appendix 3 for a list of the 100 business schools).

---

[3] See for example Pettigrew (2001), Dossabhoy and Berger (2002), Aram and Salipante (2003), March (2003), Gosling and Mintzberg (2004), Augier and Teece (2005), Bennis and O'Toole (2005), and Zell (2005).

[4] The Ecole Supérieure de Commerce of Paris (now ESCP-EAP) established in 1819, is said to be the first free-standing business school, and the Wharton School, founded in 1881, was the first school formed by a research university—the University of Pennsylvania. However, most business schools were established in the last fifty years.

[5] Available from http://rankings.ft.com/businessschoolrankings/global-mba-rankings.

To construct its table, the *FT* assigns 55 percent of weight to alumni survey returns, relying for this on criteria such as alumni salary and career progress. Twenty-five percent is put on business school characteristics—for example, measuring diversity of staff and students, and the extent to which a school is internationally recognized. A final 20 percent is allocated for research quality: here 5 percent weight is for having faculty with PhDs; 5 percent weight on the number of doctoral grads taking a faculty position at one of the world's top 50 business schools; and 10 percent weight for the number of articles in forty named academic journals.

WHERE ARE THE BUSINESS SCHOOLS LOCATED?

The international sample covers one hundred deans, two of whom are acting heads. Their scholarly backgrounds are almost exclusively in the social sciences. Because of this disciplinary homogeneity across deans, there is no need to normalize citations. Therefore, I have used raw bibliometric data, hand counted once again (from ISI Web of Science). Citations to both journal articles and monographs have been counted. Data on the one hundred deans were collected between June and July 2005, and only those deans in post during this period are included.[6]

Of the business schools in the *FT* MBA ranking (2005), 65 of the 100 are located in North America. Fifty-eight of these are in the United States, which is where most early business schools were first established. Seven schools are located farther north in Canada. There are 26 schools in European countries. Of these the majority, 14, are located in the United Kingdom. Three schools in the top 100 are in France, and there is the same number in Spain. Ireland has 2 business schools in the *FT* table, and there is 1 each in Switzerland, Netherlands, Italy, and Belgium.

Nine of the top 100 schools are spread across the rest of the world. There are 2 business schools each in Australia, Hong Kong, and Mexico. Brazil, China, and South Africa each have 1 school in the *FT* ranking.

WHO ARE THE TOP ONE HUNDRED BUSINESS SCHOOL DEANS?

There are fewer female deans in the sample of business schools than presidents in the 100 universities of the previous chapter. Only eleven deans in the *FT* top one hundred are women. Six of these are located in U.S. schools, three in the United Kingdom, and one each in Canada and Brazil. Only one woman dean runs a school in the top 20 group, unlike the position of women presidents who ran 6 of the world's top 20 universities.

---

[6] With the exception of one dean who was appointed two months after this period.

TABLE 3.1
Distribution of One Hundred Deans' Lifetime Citations

	Lifetime Citations	Top 50 B-schools	Lower 50 B-schools
Mean	355	447	263
Median	103	183	52

With regard to deans' backgrounds, nine of the one hundred have come from the business sector and not from academia, though two of the nine have PhDs. Most of the business school leaders in the sample have had traditional academic careers. Over a quarter of deans define themselves as professors of management, business administration, strategy, or entrepreneurship. In addition, there are eighteen economists; thirteen are from finance and six from accounting. Marketing professors account for seven, organizational behavior and industrial relations, six, and finally seven in operations and information management, operational research, and risk management.

Four deans running the *FT* 100 schools are highly cited (those, approximately, in the top 250 of their field), at Harvard, Wharton, Columbia, and Warwick business schools.[7] Of interest and relevance to the claims in this book is that three of the highly cited deans run schools ranked in the *FT* table at positions 1, 2, and 3.

Are Deans in the Top Schools More Highly Cited?

The individual lifetime citation scores of the one hundred deans in this study lie in the range 0 to 3,378. The figures presented in table 3.1 show the distribution of citations. In this group of deans, the mean citation score is 355 and the median score is 103. There are three deans with scores of over 2,500 lifetime citations. Twenty deans have a citation score of zero. Only four university presidents in the Jiao Tong ranking had no lifetime citations. It is useful to begin by splitting the group of deans in half.

Among those who run the world's top 50 business schools, the deans' mean citation score is 447 and the median is 183. The mean citation score of the next fifty deans is 263 and the median is 52. These data are presented as averages in figure 3.1. The bar chart shows that deans running business schools in the top half of the *FT* table collectively have just under double

---

[7] Patrick Harker at the Wharton School and Kim Clark at Harvard have since moved on to become university presidents.

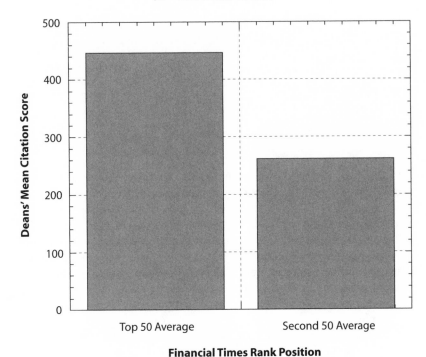

Figure 3-1. Deans in the top 50 business schools as ranked in the FT MBA league table (2005) have higher lifetime citations

the citations of those running schools positioned in the second 50 group. A pattern similar to that of university presidents in the top 100 universities clearly emerges.

The next test is to try to establish whether the relationship shown above is statistically reliable. To do this, I again use a calculation of Pearson's correlation coefficient (r),[8] in which each dean's citation score is regressed against the position of their school, to try to establish whether there is a significant correlation between the position of a school in the FT table and the citation score of a dean. The results, presented in column (1) in table 3.2, establish statistical significance at conventional confidence levels; the position of a

---

[8] The first test I apply is, again, a calculation of Spearman's rho. It tests whether the ordering of one variable (the position of a business school) is correlated with the ordering of the second variable (a dean's lifetime citations). The highest citation score is ranked 1 and the lowest is ranked 100. Using these data, Spearman's rho is 0.274. With one hundred observations, the associated 5 percent critical value for a two-tailed test is 0.195, and at 1 percent it is 0.254. Hence the correlation between leader's rank and school's rank is statistically significant at $p < 0.01$.

TABLE 3.2

Results of Cross-Sectional Correlations of Deans' Lifetime Citations by
Business School Rank from Four Different Subsamples

Pearson's Correlation Coefficient between Lifetime Citations and Rank	(1) Deans of top 100 B-schools	(2) U.S. Deans	(3) Deans from the Rest of the World	(4) UK Deans and RAE Rating
	(n = 100)	(n = 58)	(n = 42)	(n = 38)
	0.288**	0.419***	0.000	0.452**

*** p < 0.001;   ** p < 0.01

business school in the *FT* MBA ranking is associated with the number of lifetime citations accrued by its dean.

Among these one hundred deans there are three individuals with very high levels of citations. It is important to check that the results presented here are not being driven by these outliers, thereby skewing the figures. When I run the same statistical tests but remove the three outliers from the data, the correlation is in fact strengthened.[9] This shows that the highly cited leaders are not overly influencing the results.

Does the Correlation Exist in U.S. Business Schools?

American business schools dominate the *FT* MBA ranking—58 are located there. In the top 20 group, 15 are American. Once again, U.S. leaders have higher average lifetime citations than those heading schools in other parts of the world. The mean lifetime citation score of the fifty-eight U.S. deans is 449 and the median score is 210. Therefore, as with the sample of universities, U.S. business schools are selecting, on average, heads who are more established scholars. Statistical results are presented in column (2) of table 3.2. When Pearson's *r* is applied to the U.S. group, I find the correlation is again statistically significant.

These tests show that among the whole group of business schools, the higher a school is in the league table, the more distinguished is its dean as a scholar. On average, as an empirical association, six hundred extra citations will, at the mean values, move a school from the bottom of the *FT* 100 ranking to the top. The correlation holds for the full group of one hundred deans and also for the subsample of fifty-eight U.S. deans.

[9] Pearson's *r* increases to 0.351, which is now significant at p < 0.001. When the same test is applied, but this time to the logarithm of deans' citations, Pearson's *r* is 0.275, which is significant at p < 0.01.

However, when the Pearson's test is applied to the group of 43 non-American institutions only, there is no statistically significant correlation (see column [3] in table 3.2). This non-U.S. result—or more strictly nonresult—raises a number of questions. Could it be a reflection of bias of English-language or U.S. journal publishing, as raised earlier? Or do the top U.S. business schools perhaps favor research more than the non-U.S. institutions? It is not feasible to answer these questions here. But it is possible to isolate a single country from the 100 sample and run the same test to identify whether a similar pattern exists, thereby creating another opportunity to replicate these findings.

Does the Same Correlation Hold in Different Data on a Subsample of UK Business Schools?

After the United States, the United Kingdom, with 14, has the second-highest number of business schools in the *FT* top 100 table in the year of my data. By isolating UK B-Schools, I can test whether a similar correlation exists in another dataset. The United Kingdom seems an appropriate nation to focus on because language parity means that publishing and citations biases will be somewhat minimized. Also, the United Kingdom has a potentially useful objective measure of quality, namely the so-called Research Assessment Exercise. The Research Assessment Exercise (RAE) was set up by the UK government in 1986 to assess, with the aid of expert peer review, the quality and quantity of research being generated in UK universities.

The RAE Unit of Assessment (UoA) for business school submissions is "Business and Management Studies."[10] The year used is 2001, which was the last time the RAE assessment panels reported. Each submission is of a whole university department.[11] I have included 38 business school RAE submissions in this test. Thirty-six of the 38 schools are located within comprehensive universities. Only 2 are stand-alone business schools.

---

[10] RAE results available at www.hero.ac.uk/rae/Results/. For a review of UK management submissions to RAE 2001 see Bessant et al. (2003), and for a review of the journals cited in the business and management submissions in RAE see Bence and Oppenheim (2004) and Geary, Marriott, and Rowlinson (2004).

[11] Only those units of assessment that achieved a score above 4D in the 2001 RAE are included here. RAE scores range from 5A Star at the very top end with the A signifying that all staff in the field of business in a given university have been submitted for assessment. The scores go down to 1E, at the very lowest level, where E signifies that very few staff members were submitted. The reason in the present study for drawing a line at RAE grade 4 is because a quality threshold allows comparison with schools in the *FT* top 100 (2005). Of the UK business schools that made it into the *FT* ranking in the equivalent RAE year of 2001, the lowest RAE grade of a UK school included was 4D. In 2001 there were thirty-eight units of assessment in Business and Management Studies in UK universities rated 4D and above.

The next step is to examine whether a similar correlation exists between the 38 UK business schools (or units of assessment) and the research history of those deans in place in 2001. Again the lifetime citations of the thirty-eight leaders were hand counted.[12] There is no official RAE league table, so I have used each institution's result to rank the position of their school. For example, the top school, London Business School, that achieved the highest RAE grade, is ranked 1; the 2 schools that received the second-highest ratings, Lancaster Business School and Warwick Business School, are ranked 2; and so on down to those schools rated lowest in the RAE scores included here.

The maximum recorded number of lifetime citations of a dean in this sample of 38 British schools is 1,600 (the dean is an ISI HiCi) and the minimum is zero. The mean citation score of heads of submissions rated most highly in the RAE (graded in the 5s) is 379, and the mean citation score of those less highly graded (in the 4s) is 150. This implies that deans running departments in the former group are two and a half times more cited than those in the second column of departments that scored in the 4s. This can be seen in figure 3.2. Once again, thus, a correlation exists in another sample of leaders and institutions.

When the relationship between a school's RAE success and its dean's level of citations is scrutinized statistically (using Pearson's correlation coefficient), the results reveal a significant correlation (see column [4] in table 3.1). Specifically, an increase of sixty-five citations obtained by a dean is associated, in a cross-sectional sense, with a one-point move up in the RAE for a UK business school.

In this chapter, simple evidence is offered of a sort not previously documented in the research literature. It is that the better business schools are headed by more established scholars. The relationship is found among the international group of 100 business schools, it is repeated in the subsample of 58 U.S. schools, and, in a different dataset, found too for 38 UK university business schools in the 2001 Research Assessment Exercise.[13]

CONCLUDING COMMENTS

By focusing on business schools this chapter looks at leaders inside universities. Using the *Financial Times* MBA top 100 ranking, I report, again, that schools positioned higher in the league table are led by deans with higher levels of lifetime citations. This finding might not be expected in business

---

[12] Hand counting is necessary because an electronic count creates so many errors due to homonyms and other problems.

[13] The correlations are robust to the exclusion of outliers. This was also the case with a logarithmic transformation of the variables.

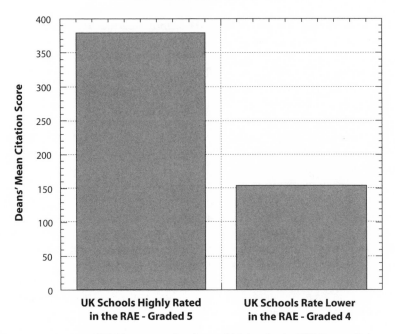

Figure 3-2. Deans of UK business schools rated higher in the UK Research Assessment Exercise (2001) have higher lifetime citations

schools, where there has been a history of appointing nonacademics into leadership positions. I also uncover this pattern in a subsample of 58 American business schools. But, again, there is no relationship among the sample of 42 schools located in the rest of the world. This result changes, however, when I isolate the United Kingdom and treat it as a separate country. In a sample of 38 UK business schools, a statistically significant correlation is reinstated. Deans leading schools that scored the highest grades in the UK's Research Assessment Exercise are considerably more highly cited than their peers in schools with less good RAE results.

The performance of a business school or university has not been shown here to be linked to the actions of a president or dean, whether highly cited or not. However, this type of research helps start the process of understanding whether there may be benefits from appointing a researcher as leader. The next chapter attempts to get closer to causal relationships.

CHAPTER FOUR

IS THERE LONGITUDINAL EVIDENCE THAT SCHOLARS IMPROVE THE PERFORMANCE OF THEIR UNIVERSITIES?

*Tis that of priority of time in the cause
before the effect.*[1]

BETTER SCHOLARS LEAD BETTER UNIVERSITIES. The earlier evidence has shown this in a variety of settings. A correlation does not prove causation, but for causation we must first have a correlation. What we do not know from the patterns presented in chapters 2 and 3 is whether more cited leaders are actually more effective. It may be that scholar-leaders are being picked for reasons other than their academic past as researchers. Scholarship might just be a proxy for management ability or leadership skills. Alternatively, elite universities, like those in the U.S. Ivy League, might choose distinguished faculty as leaders for reasons of status. But even if they do, it still seems interesting to try to understand why. Maybe all universities would like highly cited leaders but cannot afford them; maybe they would not.

In this chapter I adopt a longitudinal research design. Its aim is to try to establish whether universities that are led by more cited leaders go on to perform better in the future. I calculate each individual's level of scholarship, then, a number of years later I measure the performance of his or her institution. This relies on time lags to help uncover whether better scholars may actually *cause* research universities to improve. The issue of what is cause and what is effect is passionately debated in the social sciences. Indeed, some appear to take the extreme view that causal relationships can never be shown, and that it is almost a crime to try. Others, particularly economists, have thought a great deal in a practical way about causal associations—recently preferring to use natural or field experiments.

To truly prove causality would require leaders to be randomly assigned to universities, which would in principle make it possible to isolate the leader effect from other unobservable influences.[2] This, of course, cannot be done

---

[1] *A Treatise of Human Nature*, by David Hume (1967, p. 76), edited by L. A. Selby-Bigg. Thanks to Jeremy Miles for helpful discussion.

[2] Economists often use "instrumental variables" to try to prove causality. To get an intuitive idea of this, think of the market for corn. The outcome, the price of corn, is determined by the shape of demand and supply curves and where they cut. Rainfall, say, is a kind of instrumental variable. It shifts the supply curve of corn. As the supply curve of

in organizations, or in many other social science settings—although I do suggest in chapter 6 that there may be a great deal of randomness in the selection of leaders. In this book I take the view that we should try to get as close to a causal explanation as is possible with the available data; hence, my use of a longitudinal research design that supports the cross-section correlations and interview evidence. Later in this chapter I use multiple regression analysis to test whether university performance, the dependent variable, seems to be affected by the lifetime citations of vice chancellors, the key independent variable.

From the interviews for this book, my own experience of universities, and the many casual discussions I have had about this project, I would estimate that most faculty members believe that academics over businessmen, and more generally academics over nonacademics, are best suited to run research universities. Interestingly, it has been my experience that nonacademic staff and administrators are not so sure. I have also heard government ministers and politicians speak highly of the idea of business people running universities; and business people similarly often think they would make fine leaders. Civil servants have run a number of UK and European universities over the years, and, as suggested earlier, in the United States it has become somewhat more common for politicians to take over the top job in public universities.

Although academics usually express a preference for their peers to lead universities, when it comes to choosing an appropriate *level* of scholarship, answers are gray. I have been present when academics and administrators enthusiastically recounted stories about the inadequacies, managerial and organizational, of distinguished scholars—how many mad professors does it take to change a light bulb? and so on. When I pose the question "are all those individuals you perceive to be bad managers or leaders noted scholars?" the answer is usually no. Indeed, as suggested in the preface, it might be that good managers and leaders are distributed quite evenly among the population, whether they are journalists, janitors, or gerontologists. In the analyses in this chapter I try to uncover the approximate level of scholarship most suited to heads of research universities. It is important, again, to point out that scholarship is not being viewed as a substitute for either management experience or leadership skills.

University performance can be measured in many ways, as can leadership. The mission statements of research universities make it clear that their priorities are, fundamentally, research and teaching. However, to get appointed or promoted in these institutions it is research that is prioritized. No matter how much a university pleads for and promotes good instruction, teaching alone will rarely secure a tenured position or promotion. Institutional pres-

---

corn moves backward and forward, that variability traces out the demand curve for corn. See chapter 7 also.

tige is obtained through Nobel Prizes and groundbreaking research, not through teaching accolades. This is not to deny the importance of good instruction, only to demonstrate that research and scholarship are what distinguish top universities from their counterparts. No matter how frequently students complain about teaching playing second fiddle to research, those same individuals usually choose to have a particular university on their CV exactly because of its research reputation.

In the longitudinal results presented below, I attempt to control for other factors that might influence a university's performance. Realistically, the quality of a leader can only account for so much. The control variables I include are university income at different time periods (which is a proxy for size), the age of leaders, and their academic discipline (to identify whether there is any effect from having a scientist at the helm compared to a social scientist or someone in the humanities). These are incorporated to check the robustness of the relationship between university performance and a leader's level of scholarship. Because of the small number of observations in my study—55 universities—these are the only control variables included.

Here I use a panel of universities.[3] Institutions from the United Kingdom are used because the unique method of assessment that has been available in that country for a number of years—the Research Assessment Exercise—makes the United Kingdom a natural laboratory. It offers unusually valuable data. I observe the performance of 55 UK research universities three times in the Research Assessment Exercise (RAE)—in RAE 1992, 1996, and 2001. There are 157 university presidents, or vice chancellors,[4] in the sample who together led the 55 UK universities approximately three times in succession. Once again, the lifetime citations of vice chancellors (VCs) have been hand counted from data provided by ISI Web of Knowledge. I have normalized each leader's lifetime citations, controlling for disciplinary differences into a P-score, as in chapter 2 (see appendix 2 for information on the normalization process).

Some universities moved up in these RAE rankings more than others. The question that this chapter is trying to uncover is: have the mover universities prospered in part because their leaders were better scholars? To understand whether university performance in the Research Assessment Exercise can be explained partially by the leader-characteristic of scholarship, the study correlates a vice chancellor's lifetime citations, normalized into a P-score, with the *later* movement, up or down, in the number of excellent departments in his or her institution. In short, I try to find evidence on whether

[3] This work first appeared in a conference paper in 2007. See Goodall (2009).
[4] In this chapter where the sample of leaders is all UK-based, I refer to them as "vice chancellors" or the abbreviated version, VCs. I may also interchange with the title "president."

universities that improve in the RAE do so because they were earlier led by a distinguished scholar.

Before moving on to the statistical sections, it is interesting to first hear from the UK leaders interviewed for this book on the subject of the Research Assessment Exercise. In particular, how much do vice chancellors believe they affect their university's performance in the RAE?

WHAT THE LEADERS SAY ABOUT PERFORMANCE

When I interviewed the sample of UK university vice chancellors I asked them the question: "How much can a VC influence the Research Assessment Exercise and generally raise the research quality of a university?" There was little doubt expressed about the necessity for the vice chancellor to be centrally involved in the RAE. The responses are too numerous to present here, but a representative sample is presented.

> The VC is the only one in the university who can influence the RAE. A VC must set the quality standards and keep reinforcing them—pushing the quality line up.

One head suggested that a VC should be sacked if their university performs badly:

> A university must be prepared for it [the RAE] even though its research strategy cannot be solely designed around it. If a VC messes up in the RAE he or she should be sacked! It is the VCs responsibility to make sure that the process is done efficiently and to the best standard possible.

In the case of a university that was severely lagging in league tables and its RAE performance, a VC believed he managed to make improvements within a short period of time (of note, the quantitative evidence on his university supports this statement):

> The RAE is very important. I wanted to make X a top research university. Now it is much higher in league tables. We anticipated that it would take at least ten years but we managed to lift it in five.

Finally, many vice chancellors explained to me the processes through which a university leader can influence RAE performance—again too numerous to repeat here. Some examples include:

> The VC can have an impact on RAE by creating the right conditions, setting up the right schemes to motivate and attract the best people, offering good facilities, and creating the right environment.

This is endorsed by other heads:

> You can affect the RAE by appointing and retaining staff. I am involved with all, or most, appointments and promotions. I believe this is very important.

> The RAE is very important in appointment committees and also severance and early retirement committees. Who is entered into the RAE is decided centrally.

> I spend a large amount of time hiring people and trying to attract them. I became directly involved and managed the process of making appointments, and also internal promotions.

Vice chancellors interviewed for this study believe they play an important role in how well their universities do in the UK Research Assessment Exercise, which is the performance measure used in the longitudinal analyses. It is interesting now to find out whether a VC's own level of scholarly achievement, or lifetime citations, is correlated with RAE outcomes.

A LONGITUDINAL STUDY
OF LEADERSHIP AND PERFORMANCE

Before getting to the results, I provide a description of the data and a detailed breakdown of the performance measures. The regression equations are somewhat complex; however, I first present the findings in simple bar diagrams. The statistical results are provided later in tables.

THE SAMPLE OF RESEARCH UNIVERSITIES

There are 55 UK universities in this dataset (see appendix 3 for the full list). The institutions selected make up the oldest and most established research universities in the United Kingdom. They are often referred to as the "old" universities: those that existed before 1992, a period that marked major expansion in the number of UK higher education institutions. This group has continued to receive the bulk of UK research income and has consistently generated the lion's share of academic research.[5]

I decided, on balance, that inclusion of new universities (those established in 1992 from polytechnics) would not be appropriate. This is because in 1992, the start date in this study, polytechnics had only just formerly become universities; also, even today, despite enlargement of the sector, old universities continue to dominate the Research Assessment Exercise.

[5] Higher Education Statistics Agency (2006).

Each university in the 55 sample differs in its total revenue, age, and geographic location. Using 2001 figures, the revenue of the sample institutions ranges from £65 million ($120 million) at the lowest end, up to £450 million ($840 million) for Oxford and Cambridge. The mean revenue is £160 million ($300 million) and the median is £120 million ($220 million). There are three loosely defined categories of university in this group. The first are the universities that were established before the nineteenth century, including Cambridge, Oxford, and St. Andrews, among others. The second are the "red brick" or civic universities that were established in the nineteenth and twentieth centuries, and are located in cities like Bristol, Liverpool, and Manchester. Finally, there is a recent group of so-called plate glass universities that were established in the 1960s, and these include Essex, Warwick, and York.

Age, size, wealth, and reputation are all major contributing factors to the long-term success of a university. But it is important to mention that success over the last forty years among UK research universities has not been confined to one particular group. There has been movement up and down in RAE performance, and also in various league tables, if they are to be believed (see for example league tables in the *Guardian* newspaper and *Times Higher Education,* among others). In this study, which spans nine years, the data show that improvement in performance is not confined to the largest or the oldest institutions. Using a measure that identifies universities that have increased the number of top-rated departments over three Research Assessment Exercises (outlined below), the top 10 percent of movers up include one 1960s university and four red brick or civic universities. One is located in Wales, two in the north of England, one in the west of England, and one in the south.

The Leaders

My sample includes 157 British vice chancellors. In most cases there are three VCs per university over, approximately, a twenty-year period. Because of attempts to avoid reverse causality in the statistical calculations, it is the earlier vice chancellors who were in place in 1992 and 1996 who appear in the analysis. I have collected biographical information on each leader from "Who's Who," the Association of Commonwealth Universities, and from individuals' biographies.[6]

The focus in this chapter is on vice chancellors' lifetime citations normalized for discipline into a P-score and used as a proxy measure of each individual leader's past research productivity and influence (as outlined in appendix

---

[6] Bibliometric data on the vice chancellors was collected in October and November 2005.

TABLE 4.1
Description of the Data

	Means 1980s	1990s	2000–2005
Number of male leaders	54	54	50
Number of female leaders	1	1	5
Age of accession to leader	52 years	52 years	53 years
Leader's lifetime citations normalized into a P-score	4.59	7.80*	5.12
Length of leader's tenure	10	8	N/A
Leaders who were scientists	41	28	24
Leaders—social scientists	7	15	17
Leaders—humanities	5	10	10
Leaders—nonacademics	2	2	4
# Universities	n = 55	n = 55	n = 55

* One leader, Anthony Giddens, has exceptionally high citations. When we exclude this observation the P-score mean is 5.06.

2). A description of the information on leaders is presented in table 4.1. It is separated into three loosely consecutive time periods. This allows for a comparison among those leading the 55 research universities in the 1980s, 1990s, and early 2000s.

Gender

Immediately noticeable in table 4.1 is the small number of women vice chancellors. Of the total 157 UK leaders, over the three time periods, only seven are female. They include one woman each in the 1980s and 1990s, and five among the most recent cohort. This implies that more women are beginning to reach the top position in UK universities, even though at the end of the sample only 4 percent of the fifty-five vice chancellors are female. This figure is low when compared with the number of women presidents leading the world's top universities. As outlined in chapter 2, 15 percent of the top 100 institutions in 2004 had female presidents.

Age

Apart from sex differences, the most striking feature of the three cohorts represented in table 4.1 is in their relative similarity. For example, the mean age of accession to vice chancellor in the first two decades—the 1980s and

1990s—is fifty-two years. This age alters by a year for the 2000 cohort. In the 1960s the average age of VC was also fifty-two. Average age of accession to university leader has been rising since the turn of the century. In the 1900s, early forties was a common age of vice chancellor. By the 1950s the average age of a starting vice chancellor rose to forty-eight years, and it appears to be continuing to rise slowly. This, no doubt, partially reflects extended life expectancy.

The age pattern is replicated in U.S. data. Since 1986, the average age of college presidents has increased from 52.3 years to 59.9 years. More importantly, the proportion of presidents who were age sixty-one or older grew from 14 percent in 1986 to 49 percent in 2006, suggesting that many institutions will lose their presidents to retirement in coming years.[7]

Tenure

Length of tenure is marginally shortening. The average tenure of U.S. university leaders in the first seventy years of the nineteenth century was ten years.[8] For vice chancellors in this UK cohort, the mean length of tenure in the 1980s was also ten years. By the 1990s, the average time in office started to drop to eight years. With many contracts now renewable after five years, it is possible that the tenure of incumbent vice chancellors might decline further.

Scholar-Leaders Appear to Stay Longer

There is an interesting pattern within the data on the age of leaders. It is that vice chancellors who are more highly cited—those who have stronger research histories—appear to retain their positions as leader for longer. This is a tricky area in which to do measurements because of variation of age of retirement. In the past, UK male retirement was set at sixty-five.[9] Therefore, many of the VCs in my sample would have been forced to retire regardless of their individual contribution. Nevertheless, there is a statistically significant relationship when VC tenure is correlated with a leader's lifetime citations: the higher the citations, the longer, on average, the tenure as leader. Quite what this means is unclear. Are scholar-leaders retained by their governing bodies longer because they are better, or is it merely an illusion in the data?

---

[7] American Council on Education, The American College President: 2007 edition.
[8] Cohen and March (1974).
[9] Since 2006, UK retirement ages are negotiable in certain cases.

Academic Discipline

Table 4.1 shows that over the three decades there have been considerable changes in the disciplinary background of vice chancellors. The 1980s were dominated by scientists, who made up 75 percent of the cohort of VCs. Among the scientists the largest group at 64 percent was, overwhelmingly, engineers. In the 1980s, those with a social science background numbered only seven of the fifty-five, with even fewer, five, from the humanities. In the 1990s, scientists started marginally to reduce in numbers to 50 percent of all vice chancellors, and, of the most recent cohort, 43 percent are scientists. Social scientists as a disciplinary group have increased their presence at the top of universities, and to a lesser extent so have those from the humanities. The move away from engineers may in part be a reflection of the drop in this field of academic study in the United Kingdom and the United States, which is itself a manifestation of the downturn in engineering industries in both of these countries over the last thirty years.[10]

Nonacademic Leaders

Relevant to this study is the number of nonacademics who run British research universities. Of the 157 vice chancellors in the sample, only nine came from a nontraditional academic background. Of these, six were former civil servants; two more came from business although one, who is heavily cited, continued with research early in his career; and one leader is from a professional service firm. Glasgow University is the only institution to have appointed two civil servants out of its last three leaders.

"Career" Vice Chancellors

Finally, eight vice chancellors appear twice in this dataset. In other words, they have led more than one university in my sample between the 1980s and 2005. This group could be described as "career" VCs who may have dropped out of research at an earlier stage in their academic career to pursue administration. This is confirmed when we look at the mean citation score of the "career" group when compared to the overall citation norm of the vice chancellors. The former have half the average lifetime citations of the sample as a whole. The P-score mean for career vice chancellors is 2.4, and the median is 1.7, whereas the group mean is 5.8 and the median 5.1. Also, the average age that a career vice chancellor becomes leader is forty-eight, which is four years earlier than the group mean.

[10] Glover (1985).

UNIVERSITY PERFORMANCE—DEPENDENT VARIABLE

There are several ways to measure the long-term performance of a university. One of the most common, although possibly the least scientific, is to use league tables. As suggested earlier, the main problem with rankings is their lack of consistency in assessment methodologies. They also exclude factors such as an institution's history, reputation, and wealth. Also, most league tables are media generated, namely, they are produced by commercial organizations designed to make money by selling their publications. To create a story, the methodology is changed, often annually, which ensures that institutions at the top rotate.[11]

The United Kingdom has had a scheme for appraising research universities since 1986, one that takes place every four to five years.[12] The Research Assessment Exercise was designed to help inform funding bodies' decisions about how to distribute public money for research. Selectivity is focused on quality, in that institutions that conduct the best research receive a larger proportion of the available grant. Based on a system of peer review, the RAE provides quality ratings for research across all disciplines. Panels use a standard scale to award a rating for each submission. The ratings have changed over the different assessment exercises, but generally they range from a low of 1 to 5-star (signified here as 5*), which is the highest grade. Scores are assigned to units of assessment (equivalent to academic departments broadly speaking) depending on how much of the work is judged to reach national or international levels of excellence.[13] Submissions are then allocated a letter A–E that signifies the number of faculty in a given unit that have been submitted for review. "A" means all faculty in a given unit of assessment, or department, are being included; "D" or "E" signifies that very few are being assessed.

The UK Research Assessment Exercise is the measure of university performance used in this chapter. The RAE is appropriate because of the emphasis it places on the output of academic research, which is a core business function of research universities, the other being teaching. It is important here to mention this second core function. The quality of teaching is not being measured; however, it can be argued that there is a relationship between a university's RAE success and the standard of its instruction. In the United

[11] Lombardi et al. (2002).

[12] The strengths and weaknesses of the RAE have been hotly debated in the United Kingdom since the RAE's introduction. In interview, many vice chancellors raised criticisms, although, overwhelmingly, most expressed that despite the extra bureaucracy, the RAE had been a good thing for UK research universities. Australia is planning to introduce a similar research assessment process modeled on the UK RAE.

[13] Information about the UK Research Assessment Process is available from www.hero.ac.uk.

Kingdom the government established a separate measure to assess teaching in all universities—Teaching Quality Assessment (TQA). In this assessment process, scores are assigned to each university department based on the strength of their teaching. TQA scores have been shown to correlate highly with RAE scores.[14] In other words, those institutions that perform best in RAE tend to obtain the highest teaching quality, or TQA, scores also.

MEASURE OF PERFORMANCE

University improvement is measured here across three Research Assessment Exercises—1992, 1996, and 2001. I use it to gauge how much each university has improved or declined in the number of top departments across these periods. The focus here is on improvement in those departments that achieved the highest three scores in the RAE of 5A*, 5B*, and 5A.[15] These grades are synonymous with research considered, by peer review, to be of international excellence. Departments that achieve a top 5 grade are submitting all or most of their faculty for assessment rather than merely a portion of them, as is the case, for example, with those that get a score of 5C. Thus, it is only a part-measure of a department's quality.[16]

University performance is, then, measured by comparing the growth in the number of excellent departments—those that received a score among the top 3 grades across three Research Assessment Exercises. These figures are generated both for growth in the *number* of units and also as growth in the *changes over time* for each of the sample institutions.[17] Information on the distribution of top 5, or excellent, departments across the 55 universities is presented in table 4.2. As can be seen in the table, there is a rise in the number of submissions receiving top scores between RAE 1992 and 2001. The rise is particularly noticeable in the last time period of 1996 to 2001,

[14] See Shattock (2003).
[15] In RAE 1992 the three top scores were 5A, 5B, and 5C.
[16] Understanding the spread of grades across the RAE is helpful. In 1992 the 55 universities in this sample submitted a total of 1,799 departments. Of these, 322, or 18 percent, obtained a top score in the 5s. In the 1996 RAE the same group of universities submitted 1,761 units of assessment. In this year, of the 1,761 submissions, 525, or 30 percent, scored somewhere in the 5s between grades 5A* and 5E. Of the 525 grade 5s awarded in 1996, 320 received scores in the three top 5 grades. Thus top 5s accounted for 18 percent of the total departments submitted in 1996, whereas a third of all submissions received a grade somewhere in the 5s. In 2001, the number of 5s awarded rose even higher. In this period the sample institutions submitted only 1,676 units of assessment to the RAE. Of these, 921, or 55 percent of the total submissions, scored in the 5s, and 528, or 32 percent of the total received a top 5 grade. Therefore, with so many submissions scoring a 5 grade in 1996 and 2001, it was felt necessary to lift the threshold of performance to the top three grades awarded in the RAE.
[17] Results for the 55 sample universities on the growth in *all* grade 5 submissions over the three RAEs, is presented in appendix 5.

TABLE 4.2
Descriptive Statistics: Data over Three Research Assessment Exercises

| | (Means & Standard Deviations) | | |
Variables	1992	1996	2001
Number of top 5 departments	5.82	6.13	9.6
	(6.82)	(7.43)	(8.13)
Leader's lifetime citations	5.15	4.62	7.13*
normalized into a P-score	(7.47)	(5.94)	(21.56)
No. of Universities	n = 55	n = 55	n = 55

* One leader, Anthony Giddens, has exceptionally high citations. When we exclude this observation the P-score norm is 4.38, standard deviation is 6.92.

when the mean increases approximately a half from 6.13 to 9.6. Indeed, 55 percent of the total RAE submissions in 2001 scored somewhere in the 5s with top 5s accounting for 32 percent of all awards. The rise in the number of RAE grades at the top end contributed to my decision to focus attention on the highest scores as performance measures.

VICE CHANCELLORS' LIFETIME CITATIONS—INDEPENDENT VARIABLE

As discussed earlier, citations are references to authors in other academic papers as acknowledgment of their contribution to a specific research area. They are used in this book to signify the scholarly success of each vice chancellor. Bibliometric information has come from ISI Web of Science.

As in the previous chapter, each university vice chancellor is assigned a normalized "P-score"—vice chancellor's individual lifetime citation score normalized for discipline.[18] Table 4.2 gives a description of the data. It shows the average P-scores of leaders in the three RAE periods.

In looking at the vice chancellors' P-scores in table 4.2, a noticeable feature is the rise in mean P-score to 7.13 in the year 2001. This is due to an outlier effect, in that one leader (Anthony Giddens, Director of the London School of Economics from 1997 to 2004) has a large number of lifetime citations. As noted in the table, if the outlier is removed there is consistency in P-scores among leaders across the three time periods. The highly cited LSE head in 2001 does not influence the chapter's results because the calculations in the study allow for lags. Hence, only leaders' P-scores in 1992 and 1996 are used. The mean P-score of leaders in 1992 is 5.15 and the mean P-score of leaders in 1996 is 4.62.

---

[18] The methodology used to generate P-scores is outlined in appendix 2.

CONTROL VARIABLES—ORGANIZATIONAL REVENUE, AGE, AND DISCIPLINE OF VICE CHANCELLOR

The citation levels of vice chancellors will not, of course, fully explain leadership success and university performance. Many other factors influence the success of an institution. To try to control for some of these other factors, I include three independent variables in the statistical analysis: organizational income, the vice chancellor's age, and the academic discipline of each leader. All are measured across different time periods.

University revenue, possibly the most important control, is added for years 1992–93 and 1996–97.[19] It might be expected that a university leader is constrained by the university's finances. The income figures include government-funded grants, tuition fees and education grants and contracts, research grants and contracts, endowment and investment income, miscellaneous income, and income from services rendered.

The age of leaders is also included in the regression analysis. Finally, the academic discipline of leaders is added. Two groups are created: vice chancellors who were scientists, and those from both the social sciences and humanities.[20]

DO BETTER SCHOLARS IMPROVE THE PERFORMANCE OF THEIR UNIVERSITIES?

Here I present evidence showing that universities led by more cited vice chancellors go on to perform better in the Research Assessment Exercise. First, I collect and tabulate information about how each of the 55 universities performed in the Research Assessment Exercises of 1992, 1996, and 2001. As explained above, performance is being measured by attainment of the highest RAE grades (5A*, 5B*, and 5A). The data are then analyzed in two different ways. I start by looking at the number of excellent scores each institution acquired in the research exercises in 1996 and 2001. These numbers are then correlated with vice chancellors' normalized lifetime citations in time periods 1992 and 1996—allowing for a lag. Second, I measure the extent to which each university actually improves its performance, or not, by examining the changes in RAE scores across the three time periods. The

---

[19] It is important to note that the income variable existed only for 47 of the 55 universities. This is because no data were available to the author for the 8 University of London colleges (Imperial, London School of Economics, University College, Birkbeck, Goldsmiths, Kings, Queen Mary and Westfield College, and Royal Holloway) in 1992 when the revenue figure for each college was aggregated into one "University of London" sum. Figures supplied by the Higher Education Statistics Agency in the United Kingdom.

[20] Sciences are coded 0; social sciences and humanities are coded 1.

figures depicting institutional change in RAE, up or down, are again correlated with earlier vice chancellors' P-scores.

Central to the analysis in this chapter is the important role of time lags. These allow me to make some judgments about future performance while also somewhat protecting against reverse causality. If, for example, I include the lifetime citations of leaders in 2001, and correlate these results with performance in RAE from 1992 to 2001, then the results would not allow a causal relationship to be deduced. Causality can be more easily tested longitudinally; the action, it might be reasoned, must precede the outcome.

Before presenting the findings, I want to raise three questions that may require clarification. First, how easy or hard is it to reveal shifts in the performance of a university? The answer is that trying to explain change, or difference, is demanding. Patterns are more easily found in cross-sectional data. Measurement error is intrinsically more of a problem in change equations. This is particularly problematic for social scientists with small sample sizes, such as in a panel of 55 universities.

The second question relates to the lags in time between a change in university performance and a leader's influence: how long does it take for a vice chancellor or president to change a university? Specifically, how much time should I allow in the regression equations between the inputs of VCs' lifetime citations and the performance outputs of RAE scores? This is not a question that can ever be answered with complete accuracy. Nevertheless, in my data the minimum period is four years, between 1992 and 1996 RAE, or five years, between 1996 and 2001 RAE. Can a leader increase the number of top departments in the RAE after four or five years? The evidence presented below does suggest that there is some movement in the shorter time periods. But I believe leaders require more time to improve university performance significantly, where performance is represented in this case by attainment of the highest scores in RAE submissions. Therefore, the equations that include a nine-year lag between the input of vice chancellors' P-scores (around 1992), and the outcome of RAE grades (in 2001), may offer the most convincing evidence.

The final question pertains to the quality of each university at the start of my analysis. It asks: will the initial strength or weakness of a university not affect the ease with which an institution can change? For example, a university with 95 percent of its departments with a top grade in 1992 does not have much room for improvement. Alternatively, a university with one top department that moves to two has improved its performance by 100 percent. Later I perform a test for this, and I subsequently report that institutions that improve the most are not doing so merely because they had the furthest scope to change.

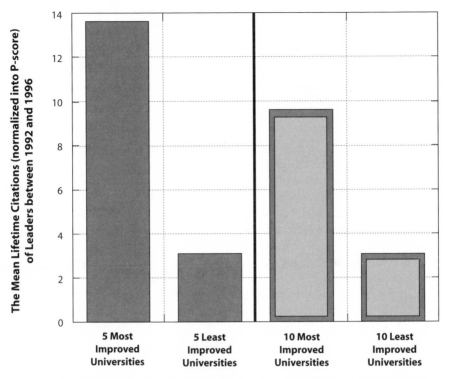

Figure 4-1. Universities that improved the most between 1992 and 2001 were led by vice chancellors with higher lifetime citations

THE FINDINGS

First, I lay out the results in simple cross-sectional bar diagrams that correlate university performance in the RAE with vice chancellors' lifetime citations. I allow for a lag. These diagrams are followed by regression equations.

The first set of results can be found in the bar diagram in figure 4.1. These suggest that the research history of a vice chancellor may affect the future performance of a university in the RAE. The focus in figure 4.1 is on the leaders of those universities that made the greatest gains, and the smallest gains, in the number of top grades achieved in RAE between 1992 and 2001. The vice chancellor's P-score figures are for the means in lifetime citations between 1992 and 1996 (thereby allowing for a lag).

As can be seen in figure 4.1, the universities that advanced the most during this period—increasing their number of excellent departments—were led disproportionately often by vice chancellors with higher lifetime citations. The mean P-score of leaders running the top five mover-universities is 13.6, while the mean P-score of those heading the top ten mover-universities is 9.6. But of the universities that accumulated the least top-fives across the nine-year period—indeed some actually reduced their number—the P-score of leaders for both the lowest 5 and 10 universities is 3.1. Therefore, vice chancellors heading the top ten mover-institutions have three times the lifetime citations of those who led universities that performed less well. Leaders in the top five best performers have over four times the lifetime citations of those running universities that improved the least.

The same pattern is captured in a second cross-sectional diagram, in figure 4.2, but this time the axes have been reversed: the X-axis gives vice chancellors' lifetime citations, again averaged between 1992 and 1996, allowing for a lag, and then ranked. Improvement in university performance in figure 4.2 is on the Y-axis. As can be seen, universities progress further under leaders with more established research histories. Figure 4.2 shows that there is a monotonic decline in the number of excellent departments as a leader's lifetime citations decline. VCs in the first column have over two and a half times the lifetime citations of leaders in the third column.

These cross-sectional diagrams with lags uncover, as a matter of statistical association, a relationship between leaders' citations and future performance in the RAE.

STATISTICAL RESULTS

In this section I report regression equations. These attempt to establish more carefully whether a statistically significant relationship exists between organizational performance, the dependent variable, and vice chancellor's P-score, among other independent variables. In the following tables the size of the effect of the independent variables is given by the coefficients, and the level of significance is given by the t-statistics. Results are presented for three time periods. The first is 1992 to 1996, followed by 1996 to 2001, and finally the full nine years, 1992 to 2001. Given the presumed importance of lags, these last results, incorporating two research exercises that span just under a decade, would seem to be the most robust.

Table 4.3 gives results for the *level*, or number, of excellent departments. It records the number of top 5s gained in 1996 in the RAE, and then reports the effects of the independent variables in 1992.

As can be seen, the P-score of a vice chancellor in 1992 is statistically significantly related to the number of top 5 departments in 1996. The coefficient is 0.30 (t-statistic = 2.29), which is significantly different from zero at the 5 percent level. Table 4.3 also shows that organizational income is statistically significant at the 1 percent level. The coefficient is 0.10 (t-statis-

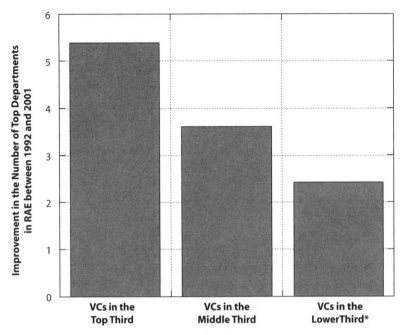

The Lifetime Citations of VCs Average between 1992 and 1996 and Ranked

Figure 4-2. Universities led by vice chancellors who were more accomplished scholars improved the most between 1992 and 2001

tic = 6.27). But age and discipline of vice chancellor are not here statistically significant.[21]

Table 4.4 gives results for the number of top 5 departments in the 2001 RAE and reports the effects of the independent variables in 1996, again allowing for a lag of five years. In 2001 the P-score coefficient is 0.53 (t-statistic = 3.04), which is statistically significant at the 1 percent level. Again, the finance variable correlates with organizational performance. The coefficient is 0.09 (t-statistic = 7.28). However, there is no statistically significant relationship with either age of leader or their academic discipline. The size of the coefficient on P-score is somewhat mediated by adding the extra variables (comparing column 1 to column 4 in table 4.4).

Table 4.5 again presents cross-sectional evidence but with a longer lag. Results are given for the number of top 5 departments in the 2001 RAE and the effects of the independent variables in 1992. This time I allow for

---

[21] When I enter P-score into the equations after the other independent variables, therefore reversing the process shown in these tables, the results stay the same. This holds for all regression equations presented in this chapter.

TABLE 4.3
Regression Equations Where the Dependent Variable Is the Number of
Top Departments in the UK Research Assessment Exercise in 1996

Independent Variables	1	2	3	4
P-score of leader in 1992	0.30*	0.21*	0.20*	0.20*
	(2.29)	(2.05)	(1.98)	(1.96)
University income in 1992/93		0.10**	0.11**	0.11**
		(6.27)	(6.56)	(6.28)
Age of leader in 1992			0.25	0.26
			(1.58)	(1.53)
Discipline of leader in 1992				0.30
				(0.16)
R	0.09	0.54	0.57	0.57
Constant	4.58	−4.55	−19.05	−19.57
	(3.87**)	(−2.71**)	(−2.05*)	(−1.97*)
n = 55				

Coefficients are shown with t-statistics in parentheses; ** p < 0.01 * p < 0.05
0 = Sciences, 1 = Social Sciences and Humanities

Table 4.4
Regression Equations Where the Dependent Variable Is the Number of
Top Departments in the UK Research Assessment Exercise in 2001

Independent Variables	1	2	3	4
P-score of leader in 1996	0.53**	0.33**	0.33**	0.33**
	(3.04)	(2.58)	(2.54)	(2.49)
University income in 1996/97		0.09**	0.09**	0.09**
		(7.28)	(7.06)	(6.87)
Age of leader in 1996			0.04	0.04
			(0.21)	(0.21)
Discipline of leader in 1996				0.11
				(0.07)
R	0.15	0.63	0.62	0.62
Constant	7.17	−3.08	−5.38	−5.61
	(5.53**)	(−1.84)	(−0.49)	(0.48)
n = 55				

Coefficients are shown with t-statistics in parentheses; ** p < 0.01 * p < 0.05
0 = Sciences, 1 = Social Sciences and Humanities

TABLE 4.5

Regression Equations Where the Dependent Variable Is the Number
of Top Departments in the UK Research Assessment Exercise in 2001

Independent Variables	1	2	3	4
P-score of leader average 1990–94	0.42**	0.30**	0.29**	0.29**
	(2.70)	(2.61)	(2.57)	(2.54)
University income in 1992/93		0.12**	0.11**	0.11**
		(6.96)	(6.95)	(6.69)
Age of leader in 1992			0.20	0.19
			(1.20)	(1.11)
Discipline of leader in 1992				−0.14
				(−0.07)
R	0.12	0.59	0.60	0.61
Constant	7.48	−2.83	−14.47	−14.21
	(5.76**)	(−1.62)	(−1.48)	(−1.35)
n = 55				

Coefficients are shown with t-statistics in parentheses;   ** p < 0.01   * p < 0.05
0 = Sciences, 1 = Social Sciences and Humanities

a lag of nine years. Here a leader's P-score, the key independent variable, has been averaged between the years 1990 and 1994. By averaging P-score over four years I hope to reduce some measurement error insofar as the results are less likely to be driven by one year of observation. Table 4.5 reports that P-score is statistically significant—at the 1 percent level—after all independent variables have been included. Again the finance variable correlates with university performance.

In terms of the size of the effect of P-score, the equation in table 4.5 illustrates that one extra point in a vice chancellor's P-score (averaged 1990–94) is associated with a rise in the number of top 5 or excellent departments in 2001 by 0.4. In other words, a hypothetical 10-point move in a vice chancellor's P-score is estimated to generate four excellent departments in 2001—or three extra departments when other variables are included. These are, of course, associations rather than clear cause and effect.

Although lags are used, the results so far are fundamentally cross-sectional. Now I turn to longitudinal analysis where the dependent variable is the change, up or down, in performance in the Research Assessment Exercise.

Table 4.6 gives regression equations in which the dependent variable is the *change* in the number of top 5, or excellent, departments, in the Research Assessment Exercise between 1992 and 1996. As can be seen in all columns in table 4.6, the association between P-score in 1992 and the later performance in 1996 is statistically significant at the 1 percent level. The coefficient is approximately 0.13 (t-statistic = 3.43). University income does not

TABLE 4.6

Regression Equations Where the Dependent Variable Is the Change in the Number
of Top Departments in the UK Research Assessment Exercises 1992–96

Independent Variables	1	2	3	4
P-score of leader in 1992	0.13**	0.13**	0.12**	0.12**
	(3.43)	(3.07)	(2.93)	(2.90)
University income in 1992/93		0.00	0.00	0.00
		(0.55)	(0.64)	(0.65)
Age of leader in 1992			0.02	0.02
			(0.36)	(0.29)
Discipline of leader in 1992				−0.11
				(−0.15)
R	0.18	0.20	0.20	0.20
Constant	−0.37	−0.61	−2.01	−1.81
	(−1.09)	(−0.90)	(−0.52)	(−0.43)
n = 55				

Coefficients are shown with t-statistics in parentheses; ** $p < 0.01$ * $p < 0.05$
0 = Sciences, 1 = Social Sciences and Humanities

now, in columns 2–4 of table 4.6, have a significant effect on the changes over time in the number of top 5 departments. It is likely that money is more significant in equations correlating P-score with the number of top 5 departments, because income is a proxy for size of an institution. A large university will tend to have more departments. When focusing on the change, however, income or size appears less important. This implies that cash is not everything.

Columns 3 and 4 show that, again, there is no well-determined effect from the age of a vice chancellor or the academic discipline to which they belong.

Table 4.7 depicts a slightly different pattern. In 2001, the number of top 5s is not strongly affected by vice chancellors' P-scores five years earlier in 1996. Although the coefficients on P-score across the four columns are insignificantly different from zero, they remain positive. Again, there is no significant effect from income or from the age or discipline of a leader.

A statistically significant relationship between performance and leaders' lifetime citations is reinstated again in table 4.8 when a longer perspective is adopted. As suggested earlier, this may be a more realistic reflection of the length of time needed to improve RAE performance. As with the previous nine-year equation, vice chancellors' P-scores have again been averaged across the years 1990–94.

It can be seen in table 4.8 that leaders' P-scores are correlated with the number of excellent departments obtained nine years later in the 2001 RAE.

TABLE 4.7

Regression Equations Where the Dependent Variable Is the Change in the Number
of Top Departments in the UK Research Assessment Exercises 1996–2001

Independent Variables	1	2	3	4
P-score of leader in 1996	0.08	0.06	0.05	0.04
	(1.03)	(0.64)	(0.53)	(0.40)
University income in 1996/97		0.00	0.00	0.00
		(0.97)	(0.86)	(0.59)
Age of leader in 1996			−0.00	0.06
			(−0.02)	(0.43)
Discipline of leader in 1996				1.97
				(1.64)
R	0.02	0.04	0.03	0.09
Constant	3.08	2.18	2.53	−1.44
	(5.07**)	(1.80)	(0.32)	(0.18)
n = 55				

Coefficients are shown with t-statistics in parentheses; ** p < 0.01 * p < 0.05
0 = Sciences, 1 = Social Sciences and Humanities

TABLE 4.8

Regression Equations Where the Dependent Variable Is the Change in the Number
of Top Departments in the UK Research Assessment Exercises 1992–2001

Independent Variables	1	2	3	4
P-score of leader average 1990–94	0. 24**	0.22**	0.22**	0.22**
	(3.27)	(2.75)	(2.76)	(2.72)
University income in 1992/93		0.01	0.01	0.01
		(1.49)	(1.30)	(1.36)
Age of leader in 1992			−0.01	−0.03
			(−0.14)	(−0.28)
Discipline of leader in 1992				−0.62
				(−0.46)
R	0.16	0.21	0.21	0.21
Constant	2.56	1.17	2.19	3.29
	(4.14)	(0.96)	(0.31)	(0.44)
n = 55				

Coefficients are shown with t-statistics in parentheses; ** p < 0.01 * p < 0.05
0 = Sciences, 1 = Social Sciences and Humanities

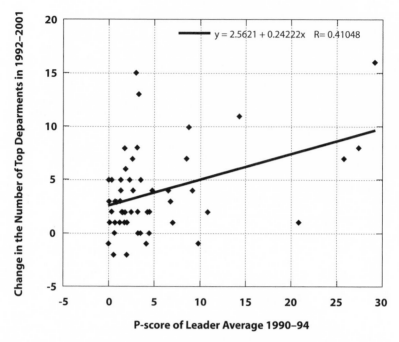

Figure 4-3. Scatter plot showing the change in the number of top departments in the UK Research Assessment Exercises 1992–2001 by a leader's P-score averaged 1990–94

The coefficient is 0.24 (t-statistic = 3.27) and statistical significance is established at the 1 percent level. Noticeably, the coefficient is double that of the 1992–96 result reported in table 4.6. Finance, age, and discipline are not correlated with university performance. In columns 2–4 of table 4.8, their inclusion in the regression equation leaves the coefficient on P-score approximately unaffected. Figure 4.3 presents these results in a scatter plot that gives each individual observation.

The results presented in tables 4.3 through 4.8 appear to demonstrate that a vice chancellor's prior success as a scholar is an indicator of the future number of top grades a university is likely to attain in the RAE. Conversely, university revenue does not affect performance. A particularly appropriate gauge of RAE performance may be to use a measure that charts the growth in departments rated excellent. Achieving the very top grades is a challenging task because excellence must be reached by almost all faculty members in a given unit of assessment. The proportion of people entered is important.[22]

_____

[22] Nevertheless, it is still interesting to look at how a university performs in the RAE in the next tier—across all five grades from A5* through 5E. These results plus analysis are in appendix 5.

As mentioned above, it might be thought that these regression equations would favor institutions that have further to move. A way to probe for this is to include a variable controlling for an institution's original position.[23] This check was done by entering the number of top 5 grades that an institution had in 1992 into a regression equation where the dependent variable is the change in top departments from 1992 to 2001. When this is done, there is no alteration in the statistical significance of vice chancellors' P-scores, or in the other independent variables of income, age, and discipline (table not reported). Therefore, institutions that improve the most are not doing so merely because they had the furthest scope to move.

A Further Check for Reverse Causality

Care has to be taken to try to check for reverse causality. This was done in the equations by introducing a series of lags between a leader being in place and the (future) performance of his or her institution. A related test, in the style of Granger causality,[24] can be applied that answers the question: are today's leaders not merely a reflection of yesterday's performance, so, for example, a distinguished scholar joins a university after, and possibly as a result of, past good performance. This causal chain is different from my hypothesis that scholar-leaders actually improve performance.

To guard against this, the leaders' P-scores in 2001 are regressed on universities' RAE performance in 1992. In an equation of this type, where the independent variable is the number of excellent top 5 departments, the coefficient on P-score has a $t = 0.80$. Thus there is no statistically significant relationship. This test goes some way to disproving the argument that the correlations in chapter 2 are merely a result of assortative matching; they are inconsistent with the objection that top universities simply select distinguished researchers as a matter of course, or because they can.

CONCLUDING COMMENTS

This chapter uses longitudinal data to explore whether the characteristics of a leader in position today can inform us about the future performance of their organization. The methodology makes it possible to go beyond elementary cross-section patterns and to try to get closer to possible causal explanations. The findings offer some of the first evidence that there may be a relationship between the research quality of a leader and later organizational outcomes.

---

[23] Thanks to Ronald Ehrenberg for this suggestion.
[24] Granger and Newbold (1974).

To perform this statistical test, unusually rich longitudinal data are needed. Here the United Kingdom provides, serendipitously, a kind of natural laboratory. My performance measure is the departmental scores achieved in the UK's Research Assessment Exercise. The dataset covers a panel of 55 UK universities—specifically, I track how each of these 55 institutions performs in the three RAEs of 1992, 1996, and 2001. When I asked vice chancellors interviewed for this book whether they believed they could influence the research performance of a university, overwhelmingly they said yes. Indeed, most expressed the view that this was uppermost among their responsibilities. A small number of their statements on this topic are recorded at the beginning of this chapter.

The lifetime citations of the sample of 157 UK university heads are again hand counted and normalized for discipline into a P-score. My hypothesis about scholar-leaders is tested by using multiple regression analysis, where university performance in the RAE is the dependent variable, and the lifetime citations of vice chancellors—normalized for discipline—is the key independent variable. Of course, the identity of individual leaders cannot solely explain organizational performance. To protect against confounding influences, I also include control variables for university income (which is a proxy for the size of the university), and the age and disciplinary background of the vice chancellor. With a small sample of universities, my control variables are necessarily few.

The results seem of interest. Using lags, they demonstrate that the universities who were led by more cited scholars went on to perform more strongly in later Research Assessment Exercises. The evidence is consistent, therefore, with the idea that having a better scholar at the helm leads to better future performance. The findings are laid out both in the form of bar diagrams, in figures 4.1 and 4.2, and in statistical regression tables, in tables 4.3 through 4.8. This does not mean that every scholar-leader turns their institution into a research powerhouse in nine years. It means that, on average, after holding constant the institution's income, or size, the age of VC and his or her discipline, there is evidence that leader-scholars seem to help the RAE performance of their universities.

The next chapter draws from interviews with university presidents and deans to try to suggest *why* scholar-leaders might make a difference to university performance.

— CHAPTER FIVE —

WHY CHOOSE LEADERS WHO ARE SCHOLARS?

WHAT UNIVERSITY PRESIDENTS SAY ABOUT IT

*The leader should represent the
aspirations of the institution.*[1]

THERE ARE A NUMBER OF MAIN SECTIONS to this chapter, and all draw
upon qualitative material from interviews with twenty-six leaders—mostly
presidents but also deans—in American and British research universities (see
appendix 1).

The interviews with university leaders seem to bring us closer to potential
explanations of the preceding chapters' data, although in order truly to
understand the transfer or "how" mechanisms, through which scholars
may actually influence performance, would require further detailed case
studies. To assess how leaders influence their organizations is inevitably challenging. This is because there is much other noise in the data, which makes
it difficult to isolate the consequences of one, albeit notable, individual.
Nevertheless, it is still interesting to hear from leaders themselves and to
conjecture why it might be beneficial for universities to select presidents
with strong research records.

The central arguments in this book about university leadership are three-
fold. First, if a university's governing body has decided upon a strategy of
raising or even *maintaining* the research quality of their institution, they
should appoint leaders who are scholars. This may not mean that every
president selected in the university's history is a notable researcher, but that
the overwhelming majority of presidents should be scholars. Second, the
appropriate level of scholarship will depend on the initial position of a given
university. For example, an institution that wishes to raise its research stand-
ing from a low base does not require a Nobel laureate as its head. This
particular argument is put most succinctly by a former university president
interviewed for this book:

> Whether a leader is an outstanding researcher or just respectable is
> relative. It depends on where an institution is and where it wants to
> be. . . . The leader should represent the aspirations of the institution.

[1] Former UK university president.

Third, in this book, scholarship is not viewed as a proxy for management experience or leadership skills. A university president must have expertise in areas other than academic research.

In the first section of this chapter, I will briefly address what some might view as the starting point—raising the question: should nonacademics lead research universities? In section two, the focus turns to the central argument in the book; specifically, it raises possible reasons why leaders who have been notable scholars might improve the performance of research universities. I propose four factors of expert leadership. The factors are partly behavioral, or internal to the leader, and partly also external, focusing on interactions between leaders and followers. How this might happen is dealt with in a later section, where I draw, again, from interview material and also the psychology literature. That segment examines the tendency of individuals to select others who are like themselves, and looks at how this human practice might affect university-faculty selection panels. Finally, I discuss the spillover effects that good scholars can create, and conclude the chapter by arguing that distinguished academics should also lead the bodies that fund research and influence university policy.

SHOULD NONACADEMICS LEAD RESEARCH UNIVERSITIES?

> To be the leader of a jazz group, you have
> to be able to play. That is true of higher
> education, as well. You might not be in
> the classroom or laboratory now, but it
> helps if you have been there.[2]

The data in chapter 2 suggested that the best research universities are disproportionately found in the United States. Knowing what differentiates these institutions from their international rivals seems especially important if universities in the rest of the world are to attain such levels of excellence and to compete for resources, and, crucially, the best faculty.

To start to answer this section's question about nonacademic leaders, it is interesting to first examine the career backgrounds of the leaders featured in this book. The great majority of the four hundred leaders in the quantitative datasets are career academics. Among presidents leading the top 100 universities in the 2004 world ranking (as discussed in chapter 2), all had PhDs

---

[2] Patrick Harker, president of the University of Delaware, and former dean of the Wharton School, University of Pennsylvania (statement available at www.udel.edu/president/leader.html).

and only two had ever worked outside academia. That the remaining 98 of the top 100 universities in the world appointed a scholar seems significant. Somewhat less surprising, perhaps, is the number of nonacademics heading business schools: of the one hundred deans in chapter 3, nine came from a business or consulting background, although two of the nine have PhDs. Finally, of the 157 UK vice chancellors featured in chapter 4, only nine, or 5 percent, are not career academics. Of these, two are from business or industry, another came from a professional service firm,[3] and six were civil servants. Thus, few research universities appear to appoint nonacademics to the top job. These revealed preferences may tell us something about what has been learned over the many hundreds of years universities have existed: that academics make better leaders.

Of the twenty-six university leaders I interviewed (see appendix 1), four did not come through the traditional academic route: Howard Davies at LSE, previously a civil servant; David Grant at Cardiff University, a former businessman; John Hood at Oxford,[4] also from business; and Richard Sykes at Imperial College London, a former businessman from an R&D background, who was, however, an active researcher throughout much of his career, and as a consequence emerges as well cited in the literature.

The notion that universities should only be led by experienced academics was a view expressed by almost all heads and deans whom I interviewed. Possibly it should be expected that presidents who are academics would speak out against nonacademics. Two leaders from nonacademic backgrounds said that it had been initially difficult for them to be accepted as head of their university. One vice chancellor described feeling like an "alien." A UK president from a business background, Richard Sykes, said that he felt he was well positioned to lead his university. He explained this was partially because he had a background in R&D, albeit in the corporate sector. Recently, however, he has stated publicly, in the *Financial Times* newspaper, that he believes business people should not lead research universities (see chapter 1).

The UK publication *Times Higher Education* (THE) ran a piece on the topic of nonacademic leaders and asked a number of vice chancellors for their comments.[5] Eleven heads responded, both from research universities and from those institutions more focused on teaching. Again, almost all vice chancellors interviewed supported the idea that academics or people with

---

[3] Professional service firms include law, accounting, consulting, and architecture practices.

[4] John Hood also led the University of Auckland in New Zealand prior to coming to Oxford.

[5] *Times Higher Education*, August 25, 2006.

knowledge of education should lead universities. One example is Terence Kealey, head of the United Kingdom's only private university, Buckingham:

> Universities should be run solely by academics. The best universities in the world are those of the American Ivy League, and they are run by academics. The connection is not hard to make.

Comments by Eric Thomas, the vice chancellor of Bristol University, are interesting. In the same issue of THE Thomas compares leadership in higher education with that in other sectors. He also suggests that Britain's National Health Service (NHS) has suffered because it placed managers, who were nonmedics, into leadership positions.

> Why are we anxious about universities being led by academics? In most sectors, chief executives have substantial point-of-service experience; why should it be any different in academe? The airline industry hires from within, as does the retail sector. A vice-chancellorship is all about leadership, and having experience of working as an academic is, I would humbly suggest, a great advantage.
>
> One of the problems in the past for National Health Service chief executives was that the majority of them did not have substantial service delivery experience—that is, only a few have been frontline clinicians as nurses, doctors, or allied health professionals. Never mind how able they are, this placed them at a disadvantage in their leadership of frontline service providers.
>
> It is healthy for the sector that most university leaders have their roots in academe. Furthermore, most will argue that higher education is one of the United Kingdom's success stories—hardly overpowering evidence of a leadership deficit.

Eric Thomas's point about the United Kingdom's National Health Service is also made by another leader interviewed for this book. This UK dean said:

> The rise of the administrator and decline of the practitioner-scholar in UK hospitals has led to an associated decline in the quality of health care.

The same dean goes on to suggest that the tide might be turning; the newly created "Academic Health Science Centre," which will be the largest NHS Trust in the United Kingdom, has been integrated with a university, Imperial College, and is being led by a noted scholar who has the joint position of CEO and principal—the first in the United Kingdom to combine responsibility for an NHS Trust with leadership of medical research and teaching in an academic institution.[6] There are signs that other trusts in the United Kingdom may follow suit.

Sir Robert May, former Scientific Advisor to the UK government and president of Britain's Royal Society, suggested in *Nature* that Prime Minister Tony Blair was overly keen on liaising with business people on matters related to universities:

> A[n] issue that has emerged during the Blair decade is the tendency to invite people from the world of business to advise on the management of universities, or to head them. Given that UK universities still stand significantly higher on international league tables than does most of the UK business sector, this seems odd.[7]

Turning to those interviewed for this study, one UK vice chancellor again compares universities with leaders in other fields:

> A successful international businessman should be appointed as CEO into an international business. An editor of the *Financial Times* will have been a competent journalist. A vice chancellor of a university must have been an academic to understand the culture. Universities are profoundly intellectual and can only be led by an academic.

A similar view is held by a former UK vice chancellor:

> Research universities should have leaders with a solid academic background and a decent publishing record. Leaders from business or politics do not work.

And from a former U.S. university dean:

> I am very opposed to appointing businessmen. I believe strongly that it is necessary to understand the culture, and also, to believe in the principle of meritocracy.

One of the presidents from a U.S. university suggested:

> Faculty at . . . would look askance if their presidents were not good academics with a research track record.

---

[6] An NHS Trust is a body created by the UK government to dispense health care services. On October 1, 2007, the Hammersmith Hospitals NHS Trust and St. Mary's NHS Trust were merged and integrated with Imperial College London. Imperial College Healthcare NHS Trust is the United Kingdom's first Academic Health Science Centre (AHSC), and will be the largest NHS Trust in the United Kingdom. The creation of a new role combines the leadership of service, research, and teaching across an NHS Trust and a university.

[7] *Nature* 447, June 2007, p. 28.

Interestingly, and possibly counterintuitively, attitudes of business school deans were comparable, albeit they had caveats. Two such opinions from deans of business schools are presented below:

> Deans from industry are a disaster. I have seen much money burned through top-down attempts to lead faculty . . . Unfortunately most MBA students want Jack Welch to be dean.

> But one former dean of the school came from a consulting firm. For the academics to accept him the school had to introduce a new academic post of deputy dean—a system that is now the norm throughout most business schools. He was considered a good dean because he came from a consulting firm where the system was similar to managing and leading faculty—leading by mutual consent, building consensus within an organization not top down. Also they have a similar promotional structure.

A similar opinion is expressed by a former business school dean:

> Business people should not lead academic business schools. It is rarely successful. There are exceptions of course, for example Wharton was once led by a former consultant. Being from a professional service firm meant that he had a better understanding of the culture than someone from another part of the business sector. But he did not get involved in any academic decisions—they were taken by a deputy dean. In my experience, business people are usually terrible teachers and they are weak speakers.

One nonacademic university head also expressed the view that he found universities to have a culture akin to professional service firms:

> Actually management problems in a university are not so different to those in other organizations. Academics aren't so different to other professional people. All are adverse to a top down style of management. I worked in a consultancy for a number of years, but I also feel that in banks it is similar. I feel that I have dealt with similar problems and cultures elsewhere.

A second nonacademic leader felt somewhat of an outsider, although he believes he was there to perform a different role from that of his predecessor.

> I still feel like an alien . . . My predecessor, who was a great scholar, united the faculty and university around the Research Assessment Exercise. But I was brought in because of my experience of mergers and also in dealing with politicians. . . . I was very surprised to be offered the job.

WHY SCHOLARS MIGHT MAKE BETTER LEADERS
OF RESEARCH UNIVERSITIES

Scholars understand other scholars. We
are part of the same tribe. A president
who is a researcher knows how to nur-
ture and protect them from the excesses
of the business model.[8]

This book emphasizes four aspects of expert-leadership—being credible, bearing the standard, having expert knowledge, and signaling priorities. However, two further explanations require discussion before getting to the core arguments. These are really statements of fact, but nevertheless they address important arguments.

The first proposes that: the earlier chapters' correlations between scholarship and leadership might be explained through unobservable heterogeneity; in other words, good researchers are simply good at everything.

If correct, this would mean that research talent is merely a correlate with or proxy for leadership ability. The positive relationship between leaders' citations and the improved position of institutions may actually be picking up a correlation between other variables. For instance, presidents who are good at research might be the kinds of people who excel in many areas of life. This is the alternative to a cause-and-effect relationship. It is also, in a sense, merely a description of the facts. But distinguished scholars undoubtedly do have tenacity, and they are often obsessive people who work long hours. Bibliometric data suggest that the highly cited are also highly productive.[9] Organizational leaders are required to have qualities of self-discipline, have an ability to work tirelessly, and be persistent and focused. Thus, this account may indeed explain some of the relationship.

The second argument is about the match between leader and university, particularly that: top institutions are more likely to seek out top scholars as presidents and deans.

It is possible that an Ivy League university automatically tends to appoint a president or dean who has either worked at an Ivy institution or studied at one. Likewise, individuals may choose to follow their peer group when applying for leadership positions. In that case there is a match between the selectors and the selected. Economists and sociologists might view this as a form of rational assortative matching—one that might represent a good

---

[8] President of a U.S. university.

[9] Lotka (1926) showed that 50 percent of the papers in physics journals were produced by 6 percent of scholars. See chapter 2.

investment return.[10] In UK universities there is little movement in vice chancellors between those leading older research universities and those in former polytechnics or recently established universities.[11]

Top universities and business schools are also well placed to attract top candidates, because they have access to greater resources and therefore can provide better facilities and salaries, although, it is important to note, university presidents' salaries do not appear to correlate with organizational performance.[12] Who gets hired to the position of dean of a business school may be a factor of the universities that house them. Schools within universities that have a strong research focus may be more likely to conform to this culture by selecting a dean who is a distinguished academic.[13] Among my sample of interviewees, Patrick Harker at the Wharton School and Kim Clark at Harvard Business School are good examples. Both are heavily cited scholars. Similarly, a leader who is a top researcher may select other top researchers into leadership positions. In short, like may appoint like (this is discussed later).

It might seem plausible that candidates' research records play a part in their selection for headship of institutions with prominent research missions. But it is also conceivable that selection committees choose almost randomly across presidential candidates' scholarly ability. Perhaps no decision is ever consciously made to select an accomplished scholar. Even if the process is arbitrary, it does not affect the empirical patterns described in this study. The longitudinal evidence presented in chapter 4 makes such a point. Universities that improved the most in the Research Assessment Exercise (RAE)—that were led by better scholars—were not among the most prestigious of UK institutions.[14]

THE FOUR FACTORS OF EXPERT LEADERSHIP: CREDIBILITY, EXPERT KNOWLEDGE, STANDARD-BEARER, AND SIGNALING

In this section I will try to uncover possible explanations for the improvements in performance of those research universities led by good scholars.

[10] Becker (1973).

[11] Bargh et al. (2000).

[12] See Dolton and Ma (2001) for UK universities, and Hallock (2002) for U.S. nonprofits. For other work on university presidents' salaries see Ehrenberg, Cheslock, and Epifantseva (2001). The average annual pay for heads of public research universities in the United States is around $400,000, and in private institutions a president is likely to earn over $700,000. In the United Kingdom, the average salary of a vice chancellor in research institutions for 2006–07 was £200,000 ($380,000).

[13] Bennis and O'Toole (2005).

[14] The top three mover institutions between 1992 and 2001 in the longitudinal study in chapter 4 are Bristol, Cardiff, and Southampton.

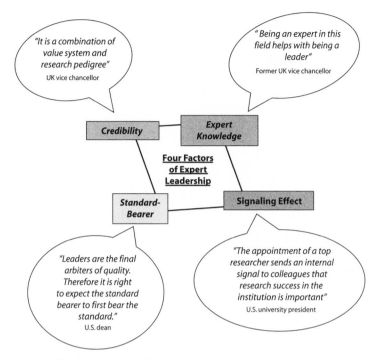

Figure 5-1. The four factors of expert leadership

I will return to the qualitative data, using illustrative accounts from interviews with leaders in universities. Often the qualitative material exceeds the space available; therefore, only a representative sample of interviewees' statements appears.

Various ideas emerge from the qualitative data—that better scholars have expert knowledge of the core business of universities, that they appear more credible as leaders, that they are standard-bearers, and that leaders who are scholars signal organizational priorities. The four factors are outlined in figure 5.1.

Credible Leadership

> You have to know the game; if not you lack credibility. Being a distinguished researcher gives you legitimacy in either a business school or a university. And legitimacy gives you authority as a leader.[15]

---

[15] Former UK business school dean and university president.

That leaders must be credible to followers was the most common assertion made by interviewees. It was suggested that, in the context of a university, an accomplished scholar communicates his or her credibility, and specifically, that he or she shares the same value system and priorities as those who are being led. As suggested by one leader, credibility legitimizes authority. This approach focuses on the social interactions between leaders and their followers.[16]

In the words of one U.S. dean:

> You need to engage the hearts and minds of faculty. Being a researcher means you have equal status, offer faculty support, speak the same language, have academic resonance and credibility, and finally, trust; trust is very important to have as a leader.

Credibility can perhaps be defined as an external factor in that others must be doing the assigning of that characteristic. Noticeably, all those who emphasized credibility and intellectual values were leaders with traditional academic backgrounds. None of the nonacademic leaders presented these kinds of arguments. The noted educationalist Birnbaum claims that presidential candidates with a traditional academic career path confer the greatest legitimacy.[17] This is particularly true for those being selected into the most prestigious institutions, which, it is suggested, are far less likely to appoint individuals from business, politics, or the military.

One U.S. university president put the same argument in terms of gaining faculty respect:

> The rationale for ranking academic excellence very highly is the enormous importance we place on the president having the respect of the faculty. Without that, it is very difficult to lead a research university.

A president being credible and also having empathy for the life of scholars was viewed as important by a majority of interviewees. Five statements are presented below; the first is from a U.S. president.

> An academic researcher-leader understands the culture of the place and particularly he or she understands the incentives. What motivates faculty and how one can get them to do what you want them to do— which is what leaders have to do.

---

[16] This approach draws from the early work of Bass (1985) and Bennis and Nanus (1985).

[17] Birnbaum and Umbach (2001). The importance of "legitimacy in the academic presidency" is also a key theme of Bornstein (2003). The idea of credible leadership is also raised by Kouzes and Posner (2003).

A UK vice chancellor said:

> It is important that a leader's value system is not too far from the values of those who are being led.

From a second UK vice chancellor:

> Nonresearchers do not have an affinity with researchers—they have little understanding of the culture, no credibility and therefore an engagement problem, and, finally, they cannot talk research.

Again, a U.S. president focuses on shared culture and values:

> The best universities tend to have the best faculty and shared values of excellent research and teaching. If the president is a scholar they have a better sense of the culture of the academy, and also they are perceived as being better able to create the right climate for academics.

The link with credibility and power is made by a UK vice chancellor:

> Having a relatively distinguished research history makes a difference to the job of VC for two reasons; you carry more weight and authority with colleagues, and second, you have an understanding of the world of research and all the pressures researchers are under.

One U.S. dean suggested that the benefits of scholarship gave him confidence as a leader:

> Being a good scholar means that I can look a Nobel or Pulitzer Prize winner in the eye. It is very important to have been a researcher or to have entered deeply into scholarly enterprise.

A head who came from business, with a strong R&D culture, again expressed a similar argument:

> When I was in industry, being a researcher there also helped with gaining credibility at many levels, because I had a particular understanding about the products and what was going on in the labs. Credibility is very important.

Very often, interviewees stated that credibility is enhanced if the head of a research university is a respected scholar. As suggested earlier, credibility is bestowed upon an individual by others. The next factor takes us inside presidents, and looks at what committed scholars actually know about the business of universities that might have come from their extended period as researchers.

Expert Knowledge

Being a good researcher I have scholarly
values, a deep understanding of the academic world, and substantial networks.[18]

This factor, expert knowledge, is internal or behavioral. I propose that, in
the context of a knowledge-intensive organization like a university, having
been an expert or top scholar provides one with a deep understanding of
the organization's core business, which may in turn helpfully influence the
behavior of leaders. Expert knowledge about research and the academy has
been learned throughout a scholar's life. It could be argued that this inherent
expertise and learning shapes the way she or he sees the world and, therefore,
affect a leader's decision-making and priorities.[19] It is also possible that having expert knowledge allows presidents, who were better scholars, to develop
superior strategies for their organization since they may be able to understand universities in ways that others cannot.

One UK vice chancellor refers specifically to his internal knowledge
and motivation:

Because I am an academic I am driven by the academy and the development of ideas and knowledge. It is my business. It is not possible for
someone external to the academy to understand this.

A statement from a former UK head illustrates this also:

I really know about the social sciences; being an expert in this field
helps with being a leader. I have mastery of the subject and therefore I
can grasp what is going on.

As does a comment from another UK vice chancellor:

I am driven by a passion for science and technology. This passion influences my world.

It is likely that top scholars have prioritized scholarship in their lives, and,
furthermore, that they may continue to emphasize activities related to scholarship once becoming a leader. Expert knowledge of the core business may
influence a leader's inherent preferences causing a scholar-leader to priori-

[18] A dean from the United Kingdom.
[19] This draws from Hambrick and Mason's (1984) upper echelons theory. UE theory
argues that top managers make strategic choices that are reflections of their own values and
cognitions, and that members of the top management team will be influenced in their
decision-making by individual and group demographic factors (such as age, education,
functional track, TMT heterogeneity, among others).

tize, over other activities, those related to research. So, for example, a president may trade off activities so that he or she can perform a central role in faculty appointments and tenure decisions, and may favor the raising of research funds over other forms of income and expenditure. Thus, a leader continues to align his or her strategic preferences with research-oriented activities once a scholar becomes head. There is evidence to suggest that strategic decisions that have been prioritized are more likely to yield successful outcomes.[20] One statement from an interview points this out:

> The best president is he or she whose scholarly priorities don't change.

The longitudinal results presented in chapter 4 might be explained by this factor. The bulk of research money from the UK government is allocated via the Research Assessment Exercise. For a university to increase or maintain its share requires dedication and focus. The central areas are in attracting new, distinguished scholars to an institution and encouraging faculty already in place to produce vibrant research. It is unlikely that a university will perform well in the RAE unless the vice chancellor makes that objective a priority. Leaders who are better scholars may be more likely to focus on the RAE. This appeared evident from my interviews with UK vice chancellors and also from the analyses of chapter 4. The top 10 percent of institutions that achieved the greatest RAE success over the period 1992–2001 were all led by distinguished scholars. Many institutions also put in place other noted scholars to head up, internally, the university's RAE strategy.[21]

Attracting and retaining outstanding faculty is central to the success of research universities. Interviewees acknowledged that accomplished or up-and-coming professors are attracted to institutions because of other top people already there.

A former UK vice chancellor said:

> When I contacted top scholars many would ask, "Who else is in the department?"

---

[20] See Hickson, Miller, and Wilson (2003).

[21] The top five movers, or 10 percent, are Cardiff, Bristol, Southampton, Sheffield, and York universities. At Cardiff University Brian Smith, a cited chemist (VC from 1992 to 2001), is credited with greatly improving research performance working with his deputy-VC for research, Hadyn Ellis, who was a renowned psychologist. At Southampton Howard Newby (VC from 1994 to 2001), a distinguished sociologist, is credited with lifting their RAE performance. At Bristol John Kingman, a distinguished mathematician (VC from 1985 to 2001), appointed Nigel Thrift, an eminent human geographer, who chaired Bristol's Research Assessment Panel from 1997 to 2001—the period that Bristol most improved in the RAE. The vice chancellor of Sheffield University 1991–2001 was Gareth Roberts, an eminent engineer and Fellow of the Royal Society; and finally, York University was led by Ronald Cooke, a distinguished geographer, between 1993 and 2002.

A second UK head commented:

> Good people only ever want to work with other good people.

One president of a U.S. university put it differently:

> Top scholars can be challenging people. They ask a lot of questions. The alternative is to shelter behind mediocrity.

Scholar-leaders are more likely to make it a priority to hire other top researchers into their university. Similarly, if an eminent academic leads an institution, it may look more attractive to new recruits. This was made clear to me when I worked with the distinguished sociologist Anthony Giddens at the London School of Economics. Not only was he obsessive about research and about hiring top scholars, but also noted academics were pleased to receive a call from him and, in many cases, be persuaded to move. This point is clearly made by a former UK head:

> A leader who is an academic helps to mobilize people. People are much more important in academic institutions than conditions. Everything in a university flows from the academic value of faculty. My priority was to ensure that we attracted and retained the best academics . . . I spent much of my time attracting good people and trying to keep our top people.

A similar comment comes from a U.S. dean:

> The most important part of the job of dean is the recruitment and retention of top faculty. Appointing good staff is the key to sustaining the position of a business school or university.

And by a UK vice chancellor:

> I have to inspire and motivate people, and to set targets—to create a supportive environment and crucially to appoint the best people.

Such a point is put succinctly by an outgoing head of a leading economics department at a UK university. Believing that a "survival guide for chairs of departments" might be helpful to others, the departing head put together a list of thirteen top tips (see appendix 6). His first is:

> Search out talent. Your first priority is to bring the best people in the world that you can to your department and try to hire them. If this takes up less than half your time, you may not be putting first things first. Your department *is* the people that you and your predecessors hired. The people that you hire will have a more lasting impact on your department than anything else you do.

One UK vice chancellor mentions the founding president of the University of California, Clark Kerr, whose obsession with appointing and retaining the very best scholars was legendary:[22]

Appointments are crucial. It's the Clark Kerr model.

It is interesting to hear from UK heads about how they directly engaged with the Research Assessment Exercise:

My own research was 5* quality and I was an expert in my field. It is very important to be a good researcher and to look others in the eye when they say they can't do something or are moaning about having to raise research funding.

These arguments suggest that having expert knowledge of the core business not only influences leader behavior toward prioritizing research and the selection of faculty, but that it may also instill the confidence to assess quality. However, it is not a zero-sum game—the false idea that more expert knowledge necessarily equals less managerial ability.

The Standard-Bearer

Leaders are the final arbiters of quality.
Therefore it is right to expect the standard-
bearer to first bear the standard.[23]

A common theme among interviewees was the importance of the leader establishing a quality threshold. The setting of an organization's academic standards was viewed as a significant part of the function of president or dean. However, a number of interviewees suggested, if you have not originally met that standard yourself, this may be difficult to enforce. Some presidents and vice chancellors also argued that it is easier to put pressure on others to perform to a high level if you, as leader, are an accomplished scholar. Such statements came only from those with traditional academic backgrounds.

One former UK vice chancellor stated:

How can you exhort others if you haven't done it yourself?

Another head made a similar statement:

My job is to lead, to represent the university internally and externally and set the quality threshold. By quality threshold I mean articulate

[22] See Kerr (2001).
[23] U.S. dean.

and decide upon what level of quality the university wants to aspire to. When a quality threshold is established, it sends out a message that no one below the threshold should be accepted into the university; it sets the quality agenda.

A U.S. president again states that in order to set the standard you must first meet them:

> My job involves broad direction-setting and imposing standards. In order to impose standards it is easier if you have first met them yourself.

A UK vice chancellor focuses on the institution's research ambitions:

> I feel that as the VC is the one who sets the quality tone for research and the strategy generally, and also is responsible for raising aspirations, it is important that he or she has been a researcher; particularly to raise the research ambition.

In my sample, a number of UK vice chancellors had continued to do research in the run up to the recent UK Research Assessment Exercise (2008), because, again, they said it set a standard. One UK vice chancellor said:

> I continue to do research now both for myself and also the signal that it sends to others. Academics find it hard to complain about combining the pressures of administration and the demands of research when they hear that I am still managing to publish research as VC.

A second UK head agreed:

> I was submitted to the last RAE, and it gave me extraordinary weight, that I could fulfill the role of VC and still submit research into the RAE. It sends a very strong message to the community.

Thus, if the head of an institution can have this effect, it makes good sense for the leader of a research university to have been a respected scholar. Also, by continuing to do research, a head enforces a second kind of standard, namely, a demonstration to faculty that despite an enormous workload they can still publish. Probably it is easier for social scientists or those in the humanities to continue with their academic work. Scientists who need labs and grant money may not have this option. This is suggested by the comment of a respected chemist who took up a leadership position:

> Once a scientist gets "off the train" it is irreversible.

Of the twenty-six leaders I interviewed, most of whom were from traditional academic backgrounds, many are still publishing.

Signaling Effect

Being a researcher sends a signal to the faculty
that you, the president, share their scholarly
values and general understanding. It also
sends an internal signal to colleagues that research success in the institution is important.[24]

Selecting a noted scholar to lead a university may send out a message to
internal and also external stakeholders. A university governing body might
wish to use the appointment to signal a change in institutional strategy, or,
alternatively, to signal that there will be more of the same. This point is
made above by a U.S. president interviewed for this study, and also by Shirley Tilghman, president of Princeton, in the *Princetonian* newspaper:[25]

By having an academic at the helm, the university is stating clearly
what it values most highly.

A former U.S. dean suggests that the signal can come from those who
select university leaders:

An appointing board can signal a sound understanding of the culture
of a research university by selecting a recognized scholar with administrative ability to a top leadership position.

These messages may be important for fund-raising, alumni relations, and
general PR. It is possible that better scholars raise more money. The data in
chapter 2 show that the top universities in the world are led by more-cited
scholars; these institutions are also the richest in the world. I have consulted
with a number of fund-raisers throughout this project, and their general
view is that presidents and faculty who are strong scholars tend to make
better institutional fund-raisers. It was suggested that noted scholars express
passion and knowledge about their work, which, they argue, is addictive and
motivating to donors. Also, scholarly presidents can creatively communicate
intellectual visions that inspire alumni to give. Lawrence Summers, Harvard's controversial and short-lived president, may have lacked managerial
sensitivity, but many reported that he had an intellectual vision second to
none, and that he was possibly one of the best fund-raisers in the university's
recent history. Larry Summers was one of the most distinguished scholars at

---

[24] U.S. university president.

[25] President Tilghman was not interviewed, however she was asked to comment on my
work in the *Daily Princetonian* (October 24, 2005). See appendix 1.

the head of the top 100 universities in chapter 2.[26] Noted academics are also likely to have raised more research funding during their careers.

Alumni may also approve of having famous scholars at the helm. Distinguished people tend to have their work profiled more regularly in the media. Arguably, individuals get positive feelings from hearing or reading about scholars from one's alma mater. Alumni also like to know that the brand value of their former university is being retained or improved. An interesting example of this is the University of Warwick in the United Kingdom. It was established in the 1960s, and, therefore, is unusually young by the standards of its competitors. Yet, it is ranked today among the top universities in Britain. Thus, the value of a Warwick degree has substantially risen over the years. Alumni benefit retrospectively from this rise.

As suggested earlier, the signal a president who is a successful research academic sends may also help in attracting faculty, particularly "stars," to a university, which has perhaps become a preoccupation the world over. It may also enhance the appeal of an institution to students. Although students value many things other than the research quality of faculty, it is again the institutional brand that ultimately draws them to a college. For instance, the brands of Harvard, Princeton, and Cornell have developed because of the quality of their faculty and research.

There is competition among students to gain a place at a top research university, and the best institutions receive the highest number of applications. Tactics have become sophisticated. For example, a student can consult with "IvySuccess," a business that describes itself as "an admissions strategy firm." Or they can purchase the book *How They Got into Harvard: Fifty Successful Applicants to Harvard Share . . .* , or if in Britain, get a copy of *Getting into Oxford and Cambridge*, and so on. Concern with a university's brand can become all consuming. If a student fails to meet a partner or spouse at college, he or she can always sign up later with one of the Ivy League or Oxbridge dating agencies.

LIKE-APPOINTS-LIKE:
WHY WE SELECT OTHERS WHO ARE LIKE OURSELVES

In this section I will draw, again, from interview material, and also turn to psychology and other literature to try to understand *how* leaders who are scholars might raise or maintain standards in universities. The main idea put forward is that people tend to select others who are like themselves. My focus is on faculty who get selected by university committees, although, interestingly, it seems there may also be like-for-like preferences in the way

---

[26] Comments are from senior fund-raisers at Warwick, London School of Economics, and Harvard.

students evaluate their university professors. Evidence suggests that under-graduates tend to prefer, and rate more highly, lecturers who have similar personality traits to themselves.[27]

This theme of like-for-like attraction was raised a number of times in interview with university leaders. The context that was being spoken about in particular is in making faculty appointments. An example of this is articulated by a UK vice chancellor:

> When it comes to making academic appointments I have found that like-appoints-like, so you must have the best faculty on selection committees. Many people who are no longer research-active tend to put themselves forward for committees. But if selection committees become too full of nonresearchers, the quality of appointments gets downgraded.

That people select others who are like themselves can be seen as another form of assortative matching.[28] It may be efficient for this to happen for individuals, but is it efficient for organizations? A statement from another UK vice chancellor suggests that it is not:

> I was recently in an appointment committee where the academic department doing the recruiting thought that they [the department] were better than anyone else did. Three candidates were short-listed. The department representatives picked the opposite order of candidates to the rest of the appointing committee. They put the worst candidate first. I think they did this because they were weak researchers and therefore lacked in confidence. Confidence is infectious.

A dean recounted a scenario that, again, appeared to be quite common among interviewees:

> The head of a physics department was ending his term. He was a middle ranking researcher, and was among other departmental faculty of about the same level or lower. The university president explained to the departmental chair that he wanted to appoint a distinguished scholar from another university who would also become the next head of department. The president consulted with the department's faculty who were not keen. Indeed, they privately telephoned the candidate and told him that "he would not be welcome" in their department. The candidate withdrew.

Although there may have been many factors involved in the decision process outlined above, the dean who relayed the event seemed to have a clear

[27] Chamorro-Premuzic et al. (2008).
[28] Becker (1973).

interpretation; he said that the department would not support the appointment because, in his view, the chosen scholar was a great deal better than the
incumbent chair and the other faculty in the department. Many interviewees
conveyed to me similar scenarios, and in my years of working with leaders
in universities I have found these kinds of situations quite common. Top
U.S. universities often employ an intervening player to control quality—
usually a dean—who has no direct link with the department making the
hire. For many of the same reasons that I argue universities should pick a
top scholar as leader, academic departments should also be led by a researcher; and in many universities this is the norm. The late Clark Kerr,
distinguished scholar and founding president of the University of California,
was a fervent supporter of selecting notable scholars as department chairs.
When Kerr was chancellor of Berkeley, he fought hard to gain the executive
power to choose department heads. It was the early 1960s, and Berkeley, led
by Kerr, was mounting a campaign to move up the league tables to the top.
He wanted to gain the highest rating for every department—which was
achieved in 1964 when Berkeley made it to number 1. A quote from this
period of change at Berkeley is noteworthy: one department head told Kerr
that "all departments had an unalienable right to be no better that they
wanted to be." Clark Kerr responded that he "accepted that 'right' only for
departments in the very top rank."[29]

The long-standing relationships between faculty members in departments
make the culture and the role of department head quite different from that
of a university president. It is harder for members of the same department
to reject a colleague's promotion or to resist hiring academics who look very
much like those already there. This helps explain why most university heads
are hired from outside a university's faculty. The tendency for academic
departments to prefer to hire others who are like them can explain why,
often, departments end up being too narrowly focused. A process that is
common among top U.S. institutions is to allow a certain amount of democracy to exist within strong departments—for example in the selection of a
new faculty member. The control of quality is then enforced one wrung up,
by a dean or provost, who, it should be noted, in the top universities is often
a distinguished scholar. He or she, with or without a hiring committee,
polices the selection and promotion process. This seems a valuable system
for two important reasons. First, the department chair can turn to his or her

---

[29] See Kerr (2001, p. 69). Kerr states that resentments to his strategies built up at Berkeley during this period. However, he also says that the Berkeley faculty, as an entirety, was
completely behind him. This is an important point; it might be difficult for a good scholar
to make major changes in an institution if the majority in it are complacent or resistant to
those changes. Hence, the importance of a strong and committed council or board. This
is discussed in the next chapter.

colleagues and "blame" decisions on outsiders, thus reducing conflict within the unit. Second, it is good for a president or vice chancellor to have an intervening quality controller, even though the president would (and should) have directly appointed that person. It is preferable for an institutional head to avoid, if possible, personally engaging in wrangles with members of departments unless it is unavoidable. At those times, it might well be beneficial for a president to take responsibility.

There are many tasks to be done in universities; some of the administrative roles may be suitable for those who have ceased, or reduced, their research. Academics' productivity may slow for different reasons—funding ceases, trends change, aging, an individual's prior work not making waves, and so on. In this book I wish to argue that *on average* those who are not active in research should also not be active on hiring committees. Exceptions to this rule might include older distinguished scholars who are still keenly in touch with their field.

The complicated topic of what motivates humans to select certain individuals over others is rarely openly discussed within universities. Yet the selection and retention of faculty is a main element in their success—as argued above. Many presidents, deans, and department heads spend much of their time on this task. Is it merely that humans find it hard to hire someone who is better than them? Maybe the selection of a better scholar alters each person's relative position within the group. A U.S. dean mentioned this scenario:

> A judicious leader is someone who is capable of hiring people smarter than themselves. I have on occasion met faculty who put the institution above their own position and chose to appoint someone better than them. But it is not common. It's a natural human reaction to find it difficult to select someone above you.

An American university president made a similar comment:

> It might be difficult for a level 2 or 3 person to appoint a level 1 person, because someone who is classed as "better" may induce negative self-feelings. Thus, we as humans may avoid such situations.

Sometimes, negative self-feelings can be traced directly to, and are antecedents of, processes of social comparison. Job satisfaction and happiness have also been shown to be related to how the self compares with similar others.[30]

In the psychology literature, self-verification theory posits that individuals need their self-view constantly confirmed, whether that self-view is positive or negative.[31] William Swann, a main proponent of the theory, said:

---

[30] Stiles and Kaplan (2004), Clark and Oswald (1996), and Luttmer (2005).
[31] Swann (1990), White and Harkins (1994).

Good researchers have positive views of their research capability, and weaker researchers have positive views of other talents, such as administration or teaching. So they may prefer similar others because they give them verification of their specific self-view, or because they have the same "shared reality"[32] in that they value the same things.

Similarly, social comparison theory purports that we assess ourselves against others, and we may do so partially in a way that leads to self-enhancement and the maintenance of a positive self-evaluation.[33] An example of this that is relevant to academics is the range of preferred options that are used to assess published work. A scholar who has many citations may tend to prefer bibliometrics, while one who has published in high-ranking journals but has few citations may emphasize journal quality, while one who appears on government committees may put much weight on that as a criterion, and so on.

The idea of "self-replication" has existed for many years, and it shows up across a number of fields, particularly biology, engineering, and computer science. Within the social sciences, the field of management has looked at issues of demographic similarity in CEO and board selection. In particular, it asks the question: do chief executives select board members who are like them and vice versa, and if so what are the consequences for CEO pay and organizational strategy?[34] There is also a range of literature focusing on diversity—ethnicity and gender. For example, in the field of law there has been debate over the composition of the judiciary and the extent to which they are reflective of society. The issue of whether representative judges are appointed to the U.S. Supreme Court has been debated since the 1930s "merit plan" and more recently in a different form in South Africa, Canada, and Great Britain, among other countries. One quote by a UK judge in an article from a law journal implies that there may be some way to go:[35]

> I would like, obviously, the judiciary to be as diverse as we can get it. But that must not interfere with the fundamental principle that we have got to choose the best man for the job.

The idea of like selecting like can, of course, be viewed as plain discrimination. When symphony orchestras change their interview procedures by using "blind" auditions with a screen to hide the candidate's identity, the probabil-

---

[32] Hardin and Higgins (1996). The statement was made through personal correspondence with William Swann, June 3, 2005.

[33] This refers to social comparison theory. See Festinger (1954), Kruglanski and Mayseless (1990), and Suls, Martin, and Wheeler (2002).

[34] E.g., Westphal and Zajac (1995) and Westphal and Milton (2000).

[35] See Malleson (2006). She quotes Lord Lloyd of Berwick's evidence to the Constitutional Affairs Committee in 2003.

ity of a woman being hired can increase.[36] The wish to select others who are like ourselves may derive from a number of motives. One idea discussed in this section is that a mid-range person is more likely to choose another mid-range individual rather than select someone ranked above them.

THE IMPACT OF GOOD SCHOLARS IN UNIVERSITIES

Most of what we know we learn
from other people.[37]

This concluding section touches upon some of the broader benefits of research universities and the leading scholars they house. As suggested in the opening chapter, universities influence local and national economies through spillover effects, which result in the growth of creativity and knowledge. Education creates human capital, which is viewed as being both internal and external; the internal benefits are localized and assist the individual, his or her family or firm, and they are paid for.[38] By contrast, the external effects—or human capital externalities—are generated through "*social* activity, involving *groups* of people."[39] This produces "free" knowledge spillovers that can disseminate widely. Research universities produce intellectual spillovers of many kinds, beyond merely those that benefit the students.

The extent to which universities engage in entrepreneurial activities varies. Sometimes a start-up is initiated by or with a university, and new product development is tied to research output. But other spillover streams exist; for example, universities are a breeding ground for informal networks and the dissemination of tacit knowledge. Another reason that employers in the knowledge-based sector may set up close to a university is the chance to employ clever graduates. Interestingly, evidence suggests that cities with large graduate populations raise the salaries of others in the area, and increase the pay of the least skilled workers.[40]

[36] Goldin and Rouse (2000).

[37] Lucas (1988, p. 38).

[38] Becker (1964). Human capital expenditures are investments in education and training. It is referred to as *human* capital because the knowledge and skills acquired by individuals cannot be removed from them in the way that their financial and physical assets can.

[39] Lucas (1988, p. 38).

[40] For the influence of human capital externalities on economic growth see Lucas (1988). For the economic effects of university or public research, see Adams (1990) and Adams and Clemmons (2008); Anselin, Varga, and Acs (1997, 2000); Basu, Fernald, and Shapiro (2001); Basu et al. (2003); Cohen, Nelson, and Walsh (2002); and Roberts (1991), Aghion et al. (2005), Stuen (2007), and Bramwell and Wolfe (2008). For a link between the location of top scientists and increases in the number of biotech firms, see Zucker et al. (1998). On how the location of university graduates increases salaries for those less educated, see Moretti (2004). For a link with top scholars and size-of-research-team effect on scientific outputs and influence, see Adams et al. (2005).

The now-famous handheld device, Blackberry, was developed by a company located near Waterloo University in Canada. One of the founders was an engineering graduate. The area around Waterloo (and there are other higher education institutions also located there) has become one of the most active high-tech hubs in Canada. The cluster of technology companies and the research of Waterloo University have now become somewhat fused. The example of Waterloo is examined in an interesting case study by two Canadian scholars.[41] They report that the university actively sought to develop industry links; it also created an innovative educational program and progressive Intellectual Property (IP) policies. However, a factor central to the region's start-up success was the academic success of Waterloo. The authors point out that the university maintained academic excellence in the areas of engineering, math, and sciences, and it worked hard to attract and retain top scientists and research students. In other words, the university appears to have focused first on its core business, and then on its commercial activities.

This point is made by the creator of the Blackberry, Mike Lazaridis, CEO of Waterloo-based Research in Motion (RIM):

> The number one reason to fund basic research . . . is to attract the very best researchers from around the world. Once here, they can prepare Canada's next generations of graduates, masters, PhDs and postdoctorates, including the finest foreign students. All else flows from this.[42]

Spillover effects can happen also at faculty level. Eminent scholars attract others, who want to work near them, and such people are also more likely to exert a pull on research funding and advanced equipment. Some evidence suggests that major scholars are able to put together larger research teams; and scientific output and influence have been shown to increase with team size.[43] The impact of "superstar" scholars has also been shown to shape the research productivity of others. This is illustrated by what happens when an eminent scholar dies: the publication output of his or her coauthors reduces substantially.[44]

There seems little doubt that prolific researchers play an important role in the world, whether as stimulants of economic growth or agents of intellectual change. Very largely, they separate the top universities from their competitors.

---

[41] Bramwell and Wolfe (2008).
[42] Lazaridis (2004, p. 8) cited in Bramwell and Wolfe (2008, p. 6).
[43] See Adams et al. (2005).
[44] Azoulay et al. (2007).

LEADERS OF ORGANIZATIONS
THAT SUPPORT UNIVERSITIES

All my life I have held the view that
universities, government research
councils, higher education bodies, trusts,
and foundations should only be led by
accomplished scholars.[45]

In this section, I extend my argument that research universities should be
led by scholars to include the case of the many other bodies central to the
survival of a productive university sector. Arguably, if President George Bush
or Prime Minister Silvio Berlusconi were outstanding scholars, the future
for publicly funded research in the United States and Italy would be dazzling.
Sadly, this is not the case. Much of the money that goes from government to
universities is tied to specific outcomes—usually political outcomes. Public
universities will always be affected by alternating governments and the
changed political priorities that brings; so too, to a lesser degree, will private
institutions, which rely on public money to fund research. In the United
States, private universities draw the largest sums from the public pot of research funding. Because of the tendency of governments to interfere with
universities (on the grounds, rightly or wrongly, that they take an amount
of public money), it seems even more important that noted scholars lead
institutions that support the sector.

Such a point was made vociferously by one of the most distinguished
university presidents I interviewed. He said:

All my life, I have held the view that universities, government research
councils, higher education bodies, trusts, and foundations should only
be led by accomplished scholars. I have said this on many occasions, in
public and private meetings, at universities and research organizations
around the world.

Established scholars, he explained, are more likely to have an informed view
and big-picture perspective about how respective scientific, and other disciplinary, fields are developing—and an ability to understand their strengths
and weaknesses, how they compare internationally, and so on. A top scholar
may also be more prepared to defend the academy against outside pressures.
At the same time, having a respected academic at the head of a funding
body, for example, may allow it to be better positioned to promote govern-

---

[45] One of the most distinguished scholars I interviewed and president of a U.S. research
university.

**Examples of Key Bodies Involved in Higher Education
Policy Making and Funding**

- In the U.S.—the National Science Foundation (NSF), National Institutes of Health (NIH), National Endowment for the Humanities (NEH), and National Aeronautics and Space Administration (NASA).

- In Europe—the European Research Council (ERC) and European Institute of Innovation and Technology (EIT).

- In the UK—the Higher Education Funding Council for England (HEFCE), Medical Research Council (MRC), Biotechnology and Biological Sciences Research Council (BBSRC), Economic and Social Research Council (ESRC), Engineering and Physical Sciences Research Council (EPSRC) among others.

- Private trusts and foundations that fund research.

Figure 5-2. Examples of key bodies involved in higher education policy making and funding

ment initiatives to the academy, as he or she is someone to whom they are more likely to listen. (Examples of the types of organizations being referred to are listed in figure 5.2.)

CONCLUDING COMMENTS

There can be exceptions to a rule or pattern. Nevertheless, this book argues that ceteris paribus—all things being equal—research universities when looking for presidents should favor scholar-leaders over managers. Using interview data with twenty-six leaders in universities, I have here tried to identify some of the possible explanations for the statistical findings in chapters 2, 3, and 4.

Why might better scholars improve the performance of their universities?

Drawing upon statements from interviewees, I began by addressing the question of whether nonacademics should lead research universities. The data in chapter 2—on presidents of the world's top 100 universities—reveal that only two leaders among this group did not come from a traditional academic background. Equivalently, among the 157 UK vice chancellors of chapter 4's analysis, only nine were not career academics. Arguably, this revealed preference tells us something important. Of those I interviewed for this study, there was consensus among those who came from a traditional academic background that business people or politicians usually do not make appropriate university leaders.

However, my main argument in this book is not that universities should be led by (any) academics, but rather that those academics chosen should be strong researchers. Why? In this chapter I return to the interview material and identify leaders' most common responses and overarching themes; these become my four factors of expert leadership. The first and most common remark from interviewees is that leaders who have been committed scholars are more credible to those inside universities. Credibility, it is argued, enhances legitimacy, and thus extends a president's power. Academic colleagues also interpret scholar-leaders as having the same values as themselves. The second factor is that scholar-leaders have greater expert knowledge of the core business of universities. I argue that not only do scholars have a deep understanding of academia, but also that a lifetime of research influences a leader's priorities. Third, many of the leaders I interviewed said that it is they who set the quality threshold in their institution, and, specifically, the standard of scholarship to which the university wanted to aspire. The bar is raised higher if a president is a distinguished researcher. One of the astute points raised, in interview, is that in order to be effective the standard-bearer must first bear the standard. The final idea to emerge from the interviews is that scholars who are leaders signal something to those within their university: research is important. This signaling effect may not just be picked up by faculty inside the institution, but also may be communicated externally, including to prospective students and to potential new hires, alumni, foundations, and the media.

At the end of the chapter, I try to home in on how scholar-leaders might effect change and improve quality. A common theme, from interviews with presidents, was that members of selection panels often choose to appoint others who are like themselves. Because like-appoints-like, it is necessary to ensure that good scholars do the hiring.

CHAPTER SIX
HOW DO LEADERS GET SELECTED?

THIS CHAPTER LOOKS at how university leaders are chosen. Universities are important institutions for the world, and I have tried to argue empirically that those who lead them make a difference to the performance of universities. Hence, leaders matter. My work attempts to reach across borders, because universities the world over have approximately the same remit. The exact methods by which leaders are selected differs across countries. Yet on average it is usual for members of university boards to hire presidents, vice chancellors, and rectors. This is also the norm in the commercial world—boards hire CEOs.[1]

In this chapter, drawing on a variety of evidence, I address two interrelated questions about the selection of leaders. First I ask: is there evidence that leaders may be chosen partially because they differ markedly from their predecessors—thus creating an alternating-leader cycle? And if so, how might this pendulum effect in turn affect an organization's strategy? For example, hiring someone who is greatly different from his or her predecessor may be efficient for a university, or alternatively it might make the long-term goals of an institution more difficult to obtain.

Using data on 157 UK university heads, I conclude that there is evidence for an alternating-leader cycle. Universities tend to switch from a stronger scholar to a weaker scholar, and then back again.

Second, using interview data with panel members of a committee set up to hire a university leader, I examine how decisions about a "person specification" are made. What sort of president does the university want to hire, and how does it come to that view? In particular, who has input into that decision? Although based only on a single case study, which may limit its applicability, my evidence suggests that the reason particular individuals are hired into the top job may be fairly arbitrary, not strategic. In the past, interesting work has been done on nonprofit and university boards that goes beyond the contribution of this chapter.[2] However, ideas on alternating leaders do not appear to have been scrutinized empirically.

---

[1] University governing boards may also be referred to as board of governors, board of trustees, board of regents, or the university council.

[2] For extensive work on nonprofit boards see Chait, Holland, and Taylor (1991 and 1996); Chait, Ryan, and Taylor (2005); and Cornforth (2005). On strategic boards see O'Neal and Thomas (1996). For recent work on university boards and governance see Shattock (2006) for the United Kingdom; for the United States see Pusser et al. (2006)

ALTERNATING-LEADER CYCLE

In interviews with me for this book, two university heads mentioned the notion that leaders alternate in character. This leads to the question: are individuals being selected in part *because* they differ sharply from their predecessors? The comments came from UK vice chancellors:

> Many places seem to have a cycle of appointing a researcher and then a nonresearcher. The selection committee that appointed me actually wanted a researcher to succeed the previous vice chancellor, who was not.

The second VC makes the same point and touches on the issue of long-term strategy:

> Institutions often fail to take the long view. They oscillate between appointing different types of leaders who push the institution in different directions.

To my knowledge, the possibility of a pendulum effect has gone largely unreported in the academic literature. The media has in the past highlighted differences between successive political leaders, and of course governments tend to swing from left to right. Anecdote would have us believe that an alternating-leader cycle seems familiar. Selection committees charged with appointing institutional heads sometimes appear, consciously or unconsciously, to be looking for "a change." It is common to hear, in general conversation, how different the new head is from the old. What does it mean if difference can be shown to be a factor common in leader selection, and how much about the new candidate can be explained as a reaction to the old? This issue is especially poignant at a time when much emphasis—some would argue too much—is placed on the desire for charismatic leaders.[3]

To establish, scientifically, that leaders alternate in character is difficult. We need to be able to identify and measure what, exactly, might be alternating. The focus in this book is on the characteristic of scholarship. Hence, I am interested in whether stronger and weaker scholars rotate, which can be done reasonably objectively using the same citations measures seen in earlier chapters. Another relevant factor might be a leader's discipline. Some institutions may feel that they have given the scientists a leader so they should now find someone in the humanities.[4]

---

and Kezar (2006); see also Birnbaum (1988), Bowen (1994), Freedman (2004), Tierney (2004), Hammond (2004), and Ehrenberg (2004). For recent work on boards and trustees across a number of sectors, see Bowen (2008).

[3] Khurana (2002).

[4] Thanks to Michael Shattock for this comment.

Any quick look at data on university presidents throws up examples of extreme switches between scholars and nonscholars. The London School of Economics replaced the most highly cited scholar in my sample, Anthony Giddens, with a former civil servant without a PhD who had never worked in a university. Harvard University replaced Neil Rudenstine, who was a lifelong university administrator, with the very highly cited, if somewhat controversial, Lawrence Summers. Sheffield University, in the United Kingdom, has systematically swung back and forth in its choice of leaders. The first of the last four vice chancellors was an unexceptional researcher, in that he was rarely cited in academic papers. He was succeeded by an exceptional scholar and Fellow of the Royal Society[5] (FRS), who was then replaced by number three, a return to a less strong scholar, only to be succeeded by their current vice chancellor who is, again, an eminent researcher and FRS. St. Andrews University, too, replaced an accomplished scientist and FRS with someone who has no research background, who is himself being replaced by a Harvard scholar; and there are many other examples. Yet, just as dice will occasionally flip from odd to even during a long sequence of throws, such patterns could be random.

While the concept of leaders alternating has received little attention in the formal literature, management scholars have written about the characteristics of CEOs, top team members, and board directors. The effect of "outsiders" versus "insiders" in CEO successions has been widely discussed; in particular, the literature contains much discussion on the shift from promoting CEOs internally to appointing them from outside the organization. The same pattern has been seen in universities. It is uncommon for a university president to be chosen from among an institution's current faculty. The possible influence of CEOs' functional backgrounds (that is, that one comes from finance or marketing), on various aspects of company strategy, corporate power and cycles of control, have also been examined extensively.[6]

The pattern I am looking to identify is whether a strong scholar—"strong researcher"—appears to be replaced by a less-cited one—"weaker researcher"—and so on, thus creating an alternating-leader cycle. To try to uncover whether there is this pendulum effect, I will return to the longitudinal data in chapter 4. This dataset allows me to examine the characteristics of consecutive leaders (the list of universities is in appendix 3). My sample is 157 vice chancellors, who between them led fifty-five UK research universities three times in succession. I observe two changes of leader per institu-

---

[5] The title of Fellow of the Royal Society (FRS) is only bestowed on individuals who are viewed as being among the top scientists in their field.

[6] For insider/outsider CEOs see Finkelstein and Hambrick (1996), and for universities see Bargh et al. (2000); for the influence of functional backgrounds see Datta and Guthrie (1994), Kim and Ocasio (1999).

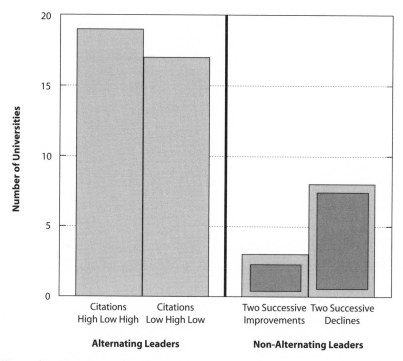

Figure 6-1. Universities that alternated between selecting a highly cited leader and a less cited leader

tion: therefore, three leaders. A small number of universities have had vice chancellors who remained in the top job for many years. These institutions have been excluded from the data because there was only one change. Thus the data include two changes of leader in forty-seven research universities. As in earlier chapters, I will identify leaders' research attainment by a P-score, which equals a president's lifetime research citations.

IS THERE EVIDENCE OF A PENDULUM EFFECT?

Do universities tend to swing from having a well-cited leader to one that is much less cited? To judge this, I calculate a Pearson's correlation coefficient. The citation scores on three consecutive leaders from forty-seven universities are studied. These generate two changes of vice chancellor per institution, thereby producing a total of ninety-four changes. The change data are what appear in the analyses and results below.

At first the data are presented in bar diagrams. There is one entry per university. In figure 6.1, I separate the VC change data into four categories. They are (i) where the first VC is more cited than the second head, who is then succeeded by a third leader with higher citations than the second; (ii) where the first VC is less cited than the second leader who has higher numbers of citations, and then the third head is again cited less than the second; (iii) where each of the leaders is successively more cited than the last person; (iv) where each of the leaders is successively less cited than the last person.

Each category is a column: the first gives the number of times when incoming vice chancellors swung from those with higher levels of citations to those with low numbers. Thus, there are nineteen universities in the sample that consistently selected leaders who alternated between a more accomplished scholar and a less accomplished one. The second category, or column, shows that seventeen universities made the alternative swing: a leader with low levels of citations is replaced by a more highly cited scholar and back again.

Columns three and four in figure 6.1 give the cases where no pendulum effect is found. The third column comprises three universities where leaders' research citations improved consecutively; here a good scholar was each time replaced by a better one. In the fourth column there are eight universities with the opposite pattern: leaders have lower numbers of research citations than their predecessors. Here there are two drops in a row.

As can be seen in figure 6.1, among the UK research universities in the sample, there is a tendency for predecessors to differ from their successors. There is a sort of "mean-reversion." Therefore, it could be that governing bodies select leaders in part *because* they differ from those they follow into the top job.

Figure 6.2 presents the same finding, but this time the data are aggregated into two columns: those institutions where a pendulum effect is found, and those that appear not to move back and forth in their choice of leader. The first column in figure 6.2 shows that in thirty-six universities, out of the total sample of forty-seven, there has been a significant switch between leaders with high citations to low, and vice versa. However, in the remaining eleven universities in column 2, no alternating-leader pattern is found.

The data in figures 6.1 and 6.2 provide some evidence that universities alternate between appointing a more established scholar and a less established one. However, is the pendulum effect statistically significant? A cross-section test is presented in figure 6.3. In the scatter plot the two changes are represented on the X and Y axes. Using Pearson's correlation coefficient (r), the degree of linear relationship between the leader changes is examined, and shown to be statistically significant. For the data in figure 6.3, Pearson's r is 0.582. The 1 percent critical value on a two-tailed test is 0.361. The size of the effect, measured by the coefficient, is 0.548, which means that the size of the change is about 0.5. In other words, leaders with greater citations than their predecessors' are followed by VCs with lower citations by approximately 50 percent.

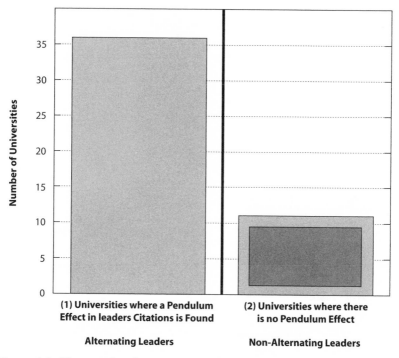

Figure 6-2. The sample of universities aggregated into those that alternate in university leader and those where no such pendulum effect is found

It is important to realize that some of the reported effect may be due to a statistical artifact caused by regression to the mean.[7] So the result might be explained, in part or wholly, by measurement error. Further replication of these UK results will, as usual, be necessary. Nevertheless, these simple tests potentially open up a new line of research, one that seems to fit the data. It appears that governing boards may select university leaders who alternate in at least one important set of characteristics—a president's level of scholarship.

DOES IT MATTER?

The idea that leaders are selected because they provide a contrast with their immediate predecessors seems logical. One leader, the incumbent, pushes the focus in one direction, which may result in other areas being neglected. Then a board selects the next head because she readdresses the balance, and

[7] Galton (1886).

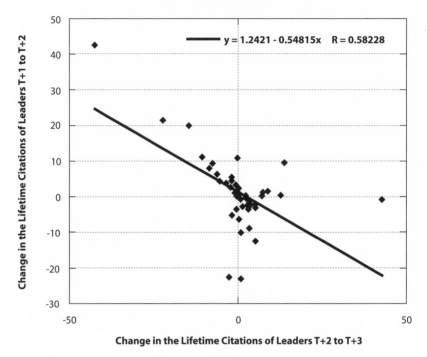

Figure 6-3. Statistical test of alternating leaders

so on. Yet a problem may arise in an organization if a new leader is appointed every few years, given quite substantial executive powers, and has different strategic priorities from his or her predecessor. What if a head proposes a substantial change for their institution, for example an acquisition or merger, or establishing a base overseas? In this case, the institution could perhaps be pulled in a number of different directions over a ten- to twenty-year period. This desire for change of direction might also come from the board members, who themselves might serve only a small number of years. What if a president has put a university on a course of substantially raising its research output or league table position? This might take many years to accomplish. Then he or she is followed by a president whose priorities are not the same. Arguably, a difference in emphasis between leaders at some level is warranted and desirable, but who ultimately is coherently steering the ship?

If there is an innate human tendency toward selecting leaders who differ from their predecessors, is this rational for organizations? It may be that the change is good for organizational performance, or it may be that it is not. This takes us into the next question about hiring university heads.

GOVERNING UNIVERSITIES
AND HIRING LEADERS: A CASE STUDY

Here I ask: is the process of choosing a leader predominantly strategic or predominantly arbitrary? In other words, are university heads hired because they fit the requirements of a long-term strategy, or are they picked more randomly and serendipitously? To address this question, I turn to two sets of interviews. First, I question the members of a panel responsible for hiring a leader for a particular UK research university, and then I present interview data from university heads about their own appointment. Again, the empirical material in this section is limited; nevertheless, the single case study throws open the lid on a procedure that is rarely written about.[8] The interviews offer a rare insight into the process of hiring a university leader, in particular, how decisions are made about the type of person chosen, and how that links in with organizational strategy. The evidence, presented below, suggests that the procedures followed by the hiring committee might be described as somewhat random, insofar as committee members appear not to have been guided by a predetermined strategy when they put together the person specification. Indeed, this point is made by one of the hiring panel members:

> The person-spec came through the consultation process, mostly the headhunters' interviews. The university had no strategy.

First some background information is necessary about the process of hiring a university president. Most universities are governed by boards, or councils. One of the main functions of a board is to appoint presidents and to monitor that leader's progress. Governing bodies are generally accepted in the literature as being "in charge" of universities in the long term. Richard Chait and colleagues suggest that, in nonprofit organizations, "in theory if not in practice, boards of trustees are supposed to be the ultimate guardians of institutional ethos and organizational values." They go on to suggest that boards are "charged with setting the organization's agenda and priorities, typically through review, approval, and oversight of a strategic plan,"[9] Boards perform broadly the same role in the private or for-profit sector. To change the direction of a research university can take many tens of years and, importantly, it also means being influenced by the strategy when appointing appropriate leaders. Of the sample of vice chancellors interviewed in this study, only one reported that his university currently had a strategy that

---

[8] One exception is the work by Khurana (2002) that offers some insight into this process in the for-profit world. Shattock (2006) also has a small section on hiring university heads.

[9] Chait, Ryan, and Taylor (2005, p. 3).

would continue beyond his own tenure as leader. This is Manchester University, which has a strategic plan that runs to 2015, although, it is important to note, Manchester's long-term strategy was likely put in place by the incumbent vice chancellor, not the board of governors.

Processes for governing executive boards have altered considerably over recent years, mostly because of corporate corruption; for example, the Maxwell affair in the United Kingdom, and more significantly the Enron and WorldCom scandals in the United States, that led to the introduction of the Sarbanes-Oxley Act of 2002.[10] The 2008 banking crash (taking place as this book was being completed) will lead to more supervision of the financial sector in particular.

Despite the increased regulation afflicting commercial boards, they still have an advantage over nonprofits. This is mainly because executive members are better represented, and commercial boards are less likely to include non-exec directors who know little about the organization's core business. Many lay people invited onto public or nonprofit boards are selected because they have influence in regional or central government circles, or because they are successful business people. The perspective and expertise that lay members bring can be helpful to universities; however, many are poorly informed about the nature of business of universities.[11] This can be a problem—one that is discussed again later.

The committees that hire vice chancellors in the United Kingdom are commonly made up of a combination of lay people, academics, and nonacademic administrators. Most are board or council members. The process is typically organized and controlled by university governors, and led by the chair of the board, or council, who is usually a lay member, and whose position is potentially vital.

Using the services of executive search firms to hire university presidents has become the norm in the United States and the United Kingdom.[12] Many universities now also employ headhunters when making other senior administrative appointments, and, increasingly, for professorial posts. Recruitment specialists have helped universities professionalize the process of hiring, and, undoubtedly, they have brought people together who would not otherwise have met. This point was made by the vice chancellor hired by the university

---

[10] For papers about the effects of the Sarbanes-Oxley 2002 Act, see Zhang (2007) and Leuz (2007) on the costs for companies of applying the legislation; about changes in board structure see Finegold, Benson, and Hecht (2007); Lorsch and Clark (2008); and Valenti (2008), and for nonprofit boards see Jackson (2006).

[11] Chait, Holland, and Taylor (1991); Shattock (2006).

[12] In Britain, according to the *Times Higher Education* and the Leadership Foundation, almost all vice chancellors hired in the past five years came through commercial headhunters (THE, November 30, 2007).

in my case study.[13] But, again, the key issue of core business is pertinent. Although the question is not answered here, it is interesting to ponder about how much knowledge those involved with recruiting heads have about the core business of universities? In particular, it seems unlikely that they understand the varied offerings from a spectrum of higher education institutions in the marketplace.

CASE STUDY OF A LEADER'S APPOINTMENT

This case study will attempt to identify whether the governors of the university in question sought to identify a candidate who fit with their long-term plans for the institution; how the decision about the candidate specification was made, and by whom; and to ascertain what criteria were used by the selection panel in making their choice.

Some detail about the participant institution is helpful.

The case study took place in a research university in the north of Britain. The selection process involved a number of stages—the first being to appoint a search company or headhunter. The headhunters, who are London based, worked with the hiring committee to develop the selection and interview program. A central coordinator throughout this process was the chair of council, a lay member, who also chaired the appointment committee.

The second stage involved communication. The chair sent an e-mail to all university staff asking them to comment on the type of leader the hiring panel should be looking to interview, and also requested potential names of candidates. Replies were then fed into the group. This was followed by a number of informational interviews, where headhunters met with a cross-section of staff, students, academics, administrators, union representatives, and council members. Interviewees were asked what they felt the university needed in its next leader. Based on the ideas generated in these discussions, suggestions were delivered from the headhunters to members of the panel.

There were thirteen people on the vice chancellor's selection committee. Four members of the panel were lay members on the university council (all were business people), one of whom was chair of council and also chair of the committee. There were three faculty members in the group, one nonacademic administrator, and a representative from the student union. Finally, in attendance, although only as observers, were three more nonacademic administrators. In this case study, I interview a number of panel members. They include: the chair and six other members of the appointment committee, three observers from the administration, the lead headhunter, and the

---

[13] In an article on this issue in the *Times Higher Education* in the United Kingdom (by Melanie Newman, November 30, 2007), a number of university vice chancellors interviewed said that without headhunters they would not have been in their jobs.

successful candidate (n = 12). In agreement with the university involved, all participants and the name of the institution will remain anonymous.

The questions I asked panel members relevant to this chapter included: Who or how did you and the hiring committee decide upon the type of person you were looking for? How much of the person specification was decided by the group, and how much of it came from feedback from outside of the hiring panel?

Interview material is presented below. Only the occupational position of each participant is identified. Each statement has been made by a different member of the committee (that is, there is one statement per participant).

According to interviewees, the person specification was put together mostly using information from the headhunter's meetings with a broad range of individuals from around the university. The recruiter explained this himself:

Headhunter:

> Input came from a bit of everywhere. We spent three days consulting with stakeholders in the university—students, academics, administrators, union representatives, council members, and the e-mail that was sent out from the chair of the selection committee.

The majority of committee members confirmed this:

Faculty member (1):

> The most important impetus came from the headhunter's one-on-one interviews with faculty. This is where the person-spec came from. There was never any agreement about it. A similar spec came from lots of sources.

Faculty member (2):

> The headhunters interviews were very important and were condensed into a useful document. The chair's e-mails were also constructive. Feedback came from Senate and Council in an understated way. Headhunters interviews were much more important.

Senior administrator, observer (1):

> The person-spec came through the consultation process, mostly the headhunters' interviews. The university had no strategy

Student union representative:

> Headhunters' interviews with people one-on-one were very helpful. The headhunters' interviews outlined what people wanted for a VC. In the first meeting we chatted about feedback. Not a lot of conversation about who we were looking for.

Senior administrator, observer (2):

> Input came mostly from two areas: from the senior academic commu-
> nity especially from individual interviews with the headhunters, and
> also from the observers.

These comments, it can be argued, identify a potential weakness in this
particular governing body's approach to hiring a leader. It would seem that
there was ambiguity about the person-spec. The board appeared not to be
marrying the applicant with a predetermined strategy (or we might expect
a clearer candidate specification at the outset). In fact, almost all of those
questioned emphasized that input came mostly from interviews and e-mails
with members of the university community. It might be fair to conjecture
that it is unlikely the CEO of a private firm, with a £400 million turnover,
would be selected by inviting comments from all staff about the type of
leader the board should appoint. Instead, one might expect a governing body
to look for a leader who matches the criteria the board believe are necessary
to develop further the university's long-term strategy. This is built into the
roles and processes of private sector boards, which have selection and recruitment as a formal part of their responsibilities (having subcommittees with
this as their sole purpose). Public universities—or publicly assisted, as is the
case in the United States and the United Kingdom—differ from for-profit
organizations because they have many more stakeholders involved; thus it is
understandable that input into the process might come from many sources.
But in this single case study it appeared that, strikingly, the selection criteria
evolved rather than were predetermined.

The chair of the selection committee and a second lay member both reported that the type of person the institution was looking for was identified
at an earlier stage.

Chair of committee, and chair of university council:

> We had quite a clear model of the type of person we wanted. This was
> created in advance. Of course humans don't all fit models exactly. We
> had a long list of what we were looking for. The input for the list and
> model came from Senate discussions and with Council members who
> were singing a similar song—researcher, researcher, researcher!

Lay member:

> It came out of the discussion beforehand. That's where the ideal type
> was decided. But you can't stick to boxes. We wanted a strong re-
> searcher.

However, these accounts conflict with the committee members' statements
above. It may be that the benefit of hindsight has contributed to their clarity;
there was a gap of approximately two months between my interviews with

panel members and their final meeting to decide the new vice chancellor. Yet even if these two members were clear in their mission, it still begs the question: why was the message not communicated to the whole committee?

Interestingly, the candidate selected to be vice chancellor also believed that she was selected according to a clear strategy by the university.

The selected candidate:

> I felt that there was unanimity in terms of what they were looking for. I felt that I fitted a template of being research active—that the university had a clear strategy.

What Was the Selection Committee Looking For in a Leader?

The desired characteristic eventually identified by most on the selection panel was that the candidate should be an academic with a strong research background. According to group members, the decision to select an esteemed scholar stemmed from discussions within the committee, from feedback from headhunter interviews, and from e-mails to the whole university inviting comment by the chair.

Senior administrator, observer (3):

> The feedback invited from the community was very helpful. A lot of people tell you what they don't want. Strong academic came out of headhunter interviews with academics, and in the e-mails.

Faculty member (3):

> A highly respected researcher was the first choice.

Administrator, member:

> We were influenced by the quality of leaders and their experience. The main information came from academic members—strong research focus and credibility. Balance between academic and leadership.

Further facts are troubling. If the desire to appoint a top scholar was so widely agreed upon, why then (as happened) did the panel select someone quite different as their runner-up candidate? Their second choice had a traditional academic background, but this applicant was not a distinguished researcher. The lifetime citations of this runner-up candidate are substantially below the average citation score of the 400 leaders included in my study. By contrast, the academic who was eventually hired as VC has a citation score far above the average among the same group. Thus, if the panel decided to select a strong researcher after a lengthy consultation process, why was their second choice so dissimilar?

In relation to the earlier discussion about alternating-leader cycles, it is interesting to note that the scholarly vice chancellor chosen by the committee contrasted substantially with the outgoing VC. That individual had stopped research early in his career so as to become an academic administrator. Interestingly, his predecessor, going back one further stage in the university's history, was another distinguished scholar.

WHAT DOES THE CASE STUDY TELL US?

This case study throws up two points. First, the evidence suggests that the selection committee chose a leader in a somewhat arbitrary fashion, as opposed to making a choice that fit with a predetermined strategy. It seems from selectors' responses above that information about the type of leader felt to be appropriate came from many sources. The most common place was from discussions between the headhunters and a broad cross-section of the university community. This perhaps means that, in practice, a university leader might be chosen based on the randomly supplied opinions of university staff and various stakeholders, instead of being selected according to criteria that link to the long-term aims of the institution. Second, with regard to the dominant characteristic or leader-type finally identified through the above process, the word *researcher* appears most often in panel members' statements to me. The appointment committee in this case study did eventually appoint a distinguished person, but the fact that the runner-up candidate had such a weak research background stands out as perplexing.

As mentioned earlier, nonprofit organizations tend to have many more stakeholders and lines of accountability than for-profits—the board, expert staff, users (that is, students and alumni), funding bodies (government and private donors)—and seeking opinions beyond the selection panel might seem sensible. It also helps to spread the word about an impending opening that may allow for more names to be thrown into the ring. The more candidates available to selectors the better; this is especially true when one considers that there are usually approximately ten vacancies for UK vice chancellors at any given time. When the chair of a hiring committee e-mails all staff and faculty in a university, it is likely to be good for public relations. Many staff members feel isolated from the workings of their institution's central administration, and they may appreciate being contacted—even if only a few actually respond (at the university in this case study, the Chair of Council e-mailed around four thousand staff, and he received forty-six responses).

Some might argue that choosing leaders as part of a strategy is asking too much of university governing boards, which typically run on goodwill and have limited availability of members. Possibly their central remit should be limited to ensuring that the right procedures are followed.

If the position of Chair of Council at research universities was an outstanding scholar, would that make a difference strategically?[14] Another question is whether university councils should ideally get more advice from their institution's most highly rated scholars. They are qualified to speak. One indirect reason to involve distinguished scholars, particularly those who have some managerial experience, rather more is that having them involved in the future of their university might increase the likelihood of them staying. Gaining their involvement on a major committee would probably require some incentives, negotiation, and as small a bureaucratic burden as possible. This discussion continues below.

What Do Leaders Interviewed for This Study Say about the Committees That Hired Them?

One former UK vice chancellor suggests that the institutional strategy was not predetermined when they hired her:

> With both chair and the committee, neither had a strategy but they had a view about what was wrong. There were 50 percent academics and 50 percent lay members plus a lay chair.

The view of a second UK vice chancellor implies they were more focused:

> The selection committee were very keen to have certain things—someone with a public profile, engagement in public policy, knowing how to manage a complex organization. Beyond that it felt quite unclear.

Signs of ambivalence about whom to choose as university leader seem clear from the next statement by the former VC of a renowned UK research university. The board's hiring committee first chose a civil servant (nonacademic) as leader, but he turned their offer down. The university then went on to select an extremely distinguished scholar, who said in interview:

> I was only appointed because their first choice turned them down—he was a civil servant.

After six years the above scholar-leader was then replaced by another civil servant—again, a leadership cycle.

A number of university heads interviewed for this study said that they felt their lay council members had very little understanding of universities. UK governing boards have been criticized for performing a weak role in protecting universities from the government policies introduced over the last

---

[14] The Chair of Council at the University of Cardiff is a distinguished scholar.

thirty years.[15] If boards will not defend universities then it begs the question, why are they there? The decline of many European research universities suggests that governing bodies have not done their job adequately. Private university boards in the United States are sometimes viewed as being more effective. A former U.S. university president made this point:

> Private universities are much better at selecting boards. They choose people who are only deemed to be good for the university.

Such a statement implies that the selection of governors onto boards in public universities may be subject to other pressures, possibly from governments. Indeed, boards of American public universities do tend to be more heavily influenced by party politics.[16] In some states—Michigan is one—the boards of the major public universities are actually appointed by the elected governor of the state. But elite private institutions can also experience conflicts between board members and faculty. This has been witnessed at the small Ivy League college, Dartmouth, where there have been disagreements about whether the college should be research oriented or instead focus more on teaching and sports. The situation at Dartmouth appears to be partially connected to the fact that a small number of board members donated large sums to the college; and consequently, they believe that given their generous contribution they should be allowed to have a say in Dartmouth's future.[17] This is an oft-debated issue among fund-raisers in charitable and nonprofit organizations that rely on donations. One of the main difficulties in relations between donors and recipient organizations is in managing the expectations that benefactors have about how their money will be spent, and about what level of involvement they can expect to have.

With regard to how well lay members on boards understand universities, one UK vice chancellor in this study put it to the test:

> Regarding the Council and how much they know about universities, we interviewed our council members and some interesting stuff came out about how little they do know. For example, one didn't even know what the Research Assessment Exercise [RAE] was.[18]

---

[15] Trow (2005).

[16] About interference from the UK government, see Lord Robert May's comments in *Nature* (vol. 447, June 28, 2007), and for criticisms of UK boards see Trow (2005). For information on U.S. public university boards, see Kezar (2006).

[17] For some information about the Dartmouth disagreement visit http://www.boston.com/news/local/articles/2007/04/03/college_trustees_clash_on_key_values/. In the end Dartmouth hired a distinguished Harvard scholar as its president.

[18] As mentioned earlier in the book, the RAE is the mechanism through which the UK government allocates the bulk of research funding to universities.

A second vice chancellor believes that part of the problem lies with lay members:

> Lay members of council and especially business people profoundly do not understand the culture and business of a university. When it comes to selecting vice chancellors, I think that lay members' judge by character not by using objective evidence.

If university boards are weak, but presidents and vice chancellors design their institution's strategy (and overwhelmingly my sample says they do), what role can the governing board play in slowing the human tendency to change direction with every new leader? Who otherwise is captaining the long-term direction of universities?[19] If it is the board members, do enough of them really know about the business of universities? My findings are potentially a matter of concern.

CONCLUDING COMMENTS

This chapter raises complex questions about the appointment of leaders and the weaknesses of university boards. The first section proposes that leaders may be selected in part *because* they differ fundamentally from their predecessors, which, in my terminology, creates an alternating-leader cycle. To demonstrate this, I examine longitudinal data on the characteristics of leaders in research universities, and focus on two changes of vice chancellor per institution. There is evidence that universities swing from one kind of leader to another: a strong scholar is replaced by a less-cited one, and then the reverse, and so on. The data show that, in thirty-six UK universities out of the forty-seven institutions in the sample, leaders alternated in type: on average a university that picked a better scholar as head in one period then retrenched in the next choice of leader. This pendulum effect seems not to have been documented in the research literature. Yet the implications appear to raise questions about whether this form of selection might affect, adversely or otherwise, organizational strategy.

---

[19] On September 6, 2008, just before the banking crash, Andy Hornby, the then CEO of Halifax Bank of Scotland (HBOS), was interviewed by the BBC's Robert Peston. There were clear signs that serious problems within the banking sector were emerging, which was why Hornby agreed to be interviewed. One statement made by the forty-one-year-old CEO (he was hired at age thirty-eight) was particularly interesting. When asked by Peston, "what had he learned from these difficult times?" Hornby responded by saying that the biggest lesson he had learned was that he should always be looking at least three to five years ahead. That the CEO of one of Europe's largest banks was not routinely looking a few years ahead is notable. One wonders, also, were the board? On the question of the book's theme of expert leaders—when Hornby was headhunted to become head of retail at the Halifax in 1999 he declared: "I don't pretend to know about pricing banking prod-

In the second section, I argue that the reason particular leaders are selected may be arbitrary, not strategic. I interview members of a vice chancellor's selection committee from a UK research university. Such qualitative data from panel members offer a rare insight into the process of hiring a university head—in particular, how decisions are made about the type of person chosen, and how the process, again, links with organizational strategy. It is only a single case study, and, therefore, not necessarily generalizable; nevertheless, it seems to expose a procedure that is seldom written about. The evidence suggests that the process followed by the hiring panel was somewhat random and the person specification appeared not to have been informed by a strategic plan.

That organizations and their governing bodies might want to consult with colleagues to inform the process of a leader's selection seems unsurprising; it may even be laudable. Universities, unlike for-profit companies, are accountable to many stakeholders. Also, if lay council members are ill informed about the core business of universities, as suggested by two vice chancellors in interview, then institutional input makes sense. But it might be thought that such a system cannot be efficient, because it depends on providence instead of planning.

The process of hiring a leader is always going to be imprecise, and more research on other universities' methods is needed. Selection criteria will include many factors, and not all of them will look rational. Nevertheless, it is questionable whether an organization with a turnover of close to $1 billion ought to select a leader based on the accumulated thoughts of a small collection of members of staff and lay board members. It would, instead, be expected that a strategic plan would inform the choice of a university leader.

---

ucts" (*Daily Telegraph*, September 18, 2008). HBOS was saved from collapse by the UK government in October 2008.

—— CHAPTER SEVEN ——
EXPERT LEADERS AMONG PROFESSIONALS, IN SPORT AND THE ARTS

> CEO is a command-and-control sort of
> position. I do not really see myself as a CEO.
> Rather, I like to think of myself as a managing
> partner. The senior partners are the faculty,
> and *they are the lifeblood of an institution.*[1]

IN MANY WALKS OF LIFE, over the last two decades, expectations about service quality have risen and greater choice has driven competition. The movement toward a more managerial culture has meant, not unnaturally, a greater focus on how to choose and train leaders, and this issue is faced by corporations, partnerships, and nonprofits. Should a U.S. federal bank select an economist as CEO or a manager? For a law firm that prides itself on offering clients the best service in Zurich, ought it bring in a managerial tier at the top or send those interested in moving from partner to senior partner on training courses? Should a National Health Service hospital in the United Kingdom be led by a health practitioner and researcher, or instead by someone who specializes in managing? Such questions confront boards in most organizations, but perhaps especially those with knowledge at their core.

This chapter touches upon the question of whether expert knowledge is relevant or beneficial to leaders outside universities—including professional service firms such as law, accounting and architecture practices, R&D units, and consulting firms. Here clients are buying individuals' expertise, but what about sports managers and coaches, and leaders in the art world? Quantitative research in this area is sparse. First, I will review a study on basketball coaches, and then, using interview material, I will discuss the relevance of expert leadership in professional service firms and arts organizations.

BASKETBALL COACHES AND EXPERT KNOWLEDGE

As everywhere, leaders matter in sports. Large sums are spent on recruiting managers and coaches, and sports coaches often command among the high-

---

[1] Patrick Harker recently left his position as dean of Wharton School at the University of Pennsylvania to become the twenty-sixth president of the University of Delaware. Harker is the most highly cited dean in my dataset.

est salaries in U.S. universities.[2] But little is known about why some are successful while others are not. In a paper with two economists[3] we ask the question, do those who were better basketball players in their youth have more success as coaches later on? The paper shows that how well a team performs in year T (now) depends on the level of attainment—playing basketball—of its coach in approximately year T-20 (twenty years earlier). We suggest that this is because the leader, the coach, draws upon his *deep* technical ability in, and acquired expert knowledge of, the core business of the sport, in this case basketball.

Basketball can be described as a setting where it is possible to measure productivity in an unambiguous way. It is an industry where there are clear objectives, team size is small, there are good measures of leaders' characteristics and performance, and objective data are plentiful. Our focus in the study is U.S. professional basketball. We measure the success of National Basketball Association (NBA) teams between 1996 and 2003, and then attempt to work back to the underlying causes. We have data on 15,040 regular season games for 219 coach-season observations, for which we compute winning percentages; in addition, we study postseason playoff success for these coaches. Perhaps unsurprisingly, a main explanatory factor is the quality of the group of players. But, less predictably, there seem also to be clear effects from the player-ability of a team's coach. Teams perform substantially better if led by a coach who was, in his day, an outstanding player.

The study's empirical contribution is to document the existence of a correlation between brilliance as a player and the (much later) winning percentage or playoff success of that person as a coach. Such a correlation, no matter how evocative of cause and effect, might be an artifact. When we probe the data, however, there seem strong grounds for believing in a causal chain. The results are presented here in figures 7.1 to 7.3.

First, we demonstrate that the correlation is robust to the inclusion of team fixed-effects and other inputs affecting team success. This means that in the statistical investigation (using multiple regression analysis) we control for things like the club's wage bill, its physical assets, and so on.

Second, once we isolate the exact years in a team's history when a new coach arrived, we find evidence of an immediate effect. The extent of improvement in the team over the ensuing twelve months is strongly correlated

[2] In 2006–07 there were two U.S. public university coaches paid over $2 million: the University of Texas at Austin, Mack Brown $2,664,000; and Virginia Tech, Frank Beamer, $2,008,000. The highest salary in 2006–07 for a president of a U.S. public university was $752,700, paid to Mark Emmert at the University of Washington. (See *Chronicle of Higher Education*, November 16, 2007.)

[3] This section draws heavily upon Goodall, Kahn, and Oswald (2008), and I acknowledge gratefully the large contributions of my coauthors Lawrence Kahn of Cornell University and Andrew Oswald of Warwick University.

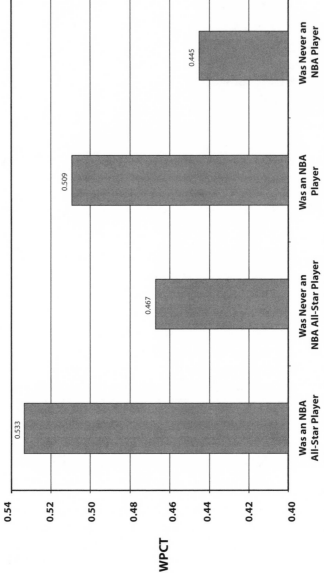

Figure 7-1. Team's regular-season winning percentage (WPCT) by coach's former NBA All-Star and player status

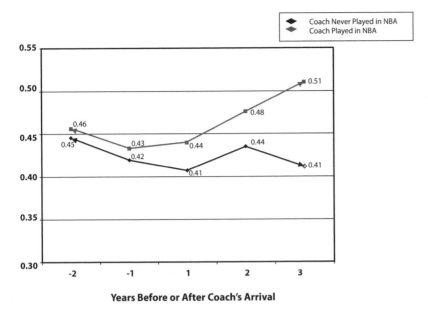

Figure 7-2. Team winning percentage (WPCT) before and after arrival of new coach

with whether the new appointee had himself once been a top player. The size of the effect is substantial: for the performance of a team, the difference between having a coach who never played NBA basketball and one who played many years of NBA All-Star basketball is, on average, approximately six extra places up the NBA league table. This is the most important finding. There is a large effect here, given the league's size of twenty-nine teams during the sample period (see figures 7.1, 7.2, and 7.3).

In complex settings it is difficult to discern a leader's input from other inputs; thus, assigning causal explanations for performance to leaders is complicated. Basketball coaches are presumably no more or less randomly assigned to clubs than are other leaders to organizations. To get around this, we use a method commonly used by economists, that of instrumental variables (IV).[4] First, we try to identify exogenous (external) variables that can be used as instruments if they correlate with the independent variable, which is the one we are trying to explain. An example we use is the birthplace of coaches, which is viewed as random. Where a coach is born might influence their choice of team, but the birthplace of a coach should make no difference to a coach's performance at the club. Two other instrumental variables used are a coaches' height and their former position on the court. Again, these

---

[4] Mendelian randomization is a similar technique used by epidemiologists.

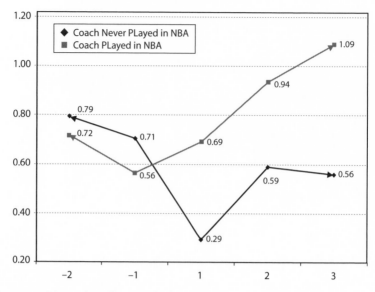

Figure 7-3. Team playoff success before and after arrival of new coach

variables might be correlated with the number of years a coach played basketball, or their level of achievement as a player, but they are unlikely decades later to affect the winning success of coaches.

When instrumental variable estimation is done, robust results are found. In the study we show that the "expert knowledge" effect appears to be large, and, significantly, to be visible in the data within the first year of a new coach arriving.

Might it be that the level of a coach's acquired skill and deep knowledge is not truly the driving force behind these results, but rather merely that some "tenacious personality" factor (or even a genetic component) is at work here, and this is merely correlated with both a person's success as a coach and having been a top player in his youth? It could. But there are reasons to be cautious of such an explanation. One is that it is hard to see why mystery personality factor X should not be found equally often among those particular coaches—all remarkable and extraordinarily energetic individuals—who did not achieve such heights as players. A second is that every social-science discovery is subject to some version of this—essentially unfalsifiable—claim. A third is that we have found that extra years of the "treatment" are apparently related in a dose-response way to the degree of success of the individual. In short, the more years as a player, the better the performance as a coach. This is a particularly important finding.

In my study with colleagues Kahn and Oswald, we try to explain our result using the same arguments that I raise about scholarly leadership in research universities in chapter 5. First, we suggest that great players have a deep knowledge of the game and can impart that to the players they coach. It is also possible that this expert knowledge allows coaches who were top players to work out better strategies, since they may be able to understand the game in ways that many, without the accumulated experience, cannot. Second, we argue that outstanding players may provide more credible leadership than those coaches who had not been really good basketball players. This factor may even be particularly important in the NBA where there are only a few hundred players in the top teams and these are recruited by searching among a global supply of thousands of fine players. Top players earn an average of \$4–\$5 million per year.[5] We surmise in the study that to command the attention of such people may take a former expert player to be a kind of standard-bearer, who can best extract effort from his players. Third, in addition to signaling to current team members that the owner is serious about performance by hiring someone who was once an excellent player, there may also be an external signaling role. Having as a coach someone who was a talented player may make it easier for the team to recruit outstanding talent from other basketball teams and countries.

In concluding, the Goodall-Kahn-Oswald paper's results demonstrate that expert knowledge may also be relevant in the sports arena. Undoubtedly, there will be some variation across different sports that future research may uncover. The next section looks at different kinds of specialist workers.

PROFESSIONAL SERVICE FIRMS

Professional service firms include those of lawyers, architects, consultants, and accountants.[6] These are knowledge-intensive organizations in which the majority of employees are experts or professionals and the most important input or stock is knowledge. As mentioned earlier, universities also fall into this category. Experts and professionals are often described as being self-motivated, preferring to work autonomously, and requiring minimal individual managing. The culture in professional service firms is collegiate, and a leader is considered to be the "first among equals." Finally, in these types of firms only those who have been successful in a professional capacity (that

---

[5] See, for the example the *USA Today* salaries database at http://content.usatoday.com/sports/basketball/nba/salaries/default.aspx.

[6] The authors who have written most extensively about professional service firms are David Maister (1993) and McKenna and Maister (2002). See also Lowendahl (1997) and Fenton and Pettigrew (2006). For work more generally on knowledge-intensive organizations see Alvesson (1992, 2004), and Alvesson and Sveningsson (2003). On project leaders in R&D firms see Narayanan (2001). On a related topic, Batt (2001) looks at teams of technicians. Goffee and Jones (2007) focus on what leaders should do to retain and encourage their "clever people" in a number of commercial settings.

is, they have excelled in consulting, as lawyers and accountants, and so on) will be accepted as leaders and managers. This is because a leader's peers will be more willing to accept someone with a strong professional reputation. Similarly, R&D project heads tend to be selected for their technical expertise as much as for their leadership skills.[7]

I raised these issues with a small number of professionals interviewed for this book (see appendix 1 for list of interviewees).

Professional service firms are normally led by one of their own: a partner or director who first proved herself or himself as an expert, but who also expressed interest in taking a leadership route and has the ability to be a competent manager. A senior director in a consulting firm makes this point:[8]

> It would not be possible to get promoted without being a good economist. This is because you have to know, at a high level, the stuff you are selling. People would ask how you did it if you got promoted without expert knowledge. But being an expert is not alone enough; a consultant must be able to develop a business practice also, and therefore they must have management skills.

He goes on to talk about presidents in his firm:

> The company president needs to be intellectually credible, as well as a good manager and leader. To date, all our presidents have been experts. Our current president continues to retain a successful consulting business, as did his two predecessors. He performs the role of president on a part-time basis. It is very important that heads continue to practice, because the value of the firm is largely made up of the intellectual capital and reputations of its experts. Also, the consultants in the firm do not see great worth in paying for full-time management.

The UK head of one of the world's largest consulting firms agrees, while also suggesting that management and leadership should viewed as being different:

> A large percentage of those who become great client people will also prove to be great managers too. These are smart individuals who can learn quickly. If you have been a successful client partner you will gain the respect of your colleagues—which you need if you are to become a leader. To lead an organization you must be seen as credible by your peers, which means in our business, having made a mark as a partner in client work.

---

[7] Handy (1984); Starbuck (1992); Maister (1993); Mintzberg, Quinn, and Ghoshal (1995); Lowendahl (1997); Alvesson and Sveningsson (2003); and Narayanan (2001).

[8] See appendix 1 for the list of interviewees.

It is important to distinguish between leadership and management. To lead you don't necessarily need to be a great manager. Often you find that individuals are good leaders but not necessarily good managers. They can run very successful teams, as long as they recognize their weaknesses and employ good managers to run the infrastructure.

The situation in law firms is described as being similar:

Most law firms are managed internally by partners. Large practices like ours will have more formal management structures. Occasionally a law firm will experiment and actually appoint a manager [someone from outside who is not a lawyer] into a senior managerial position; but the one firm I know that tried this, reverted back to the old system quite quickly. Positions like financial directors are hired externally, and they are not expected to be lawyers.

If professionals take on too much administration it can be detrimental to their reputation, as one consultant explained:

Sometimes, the Head of Office, who acts as liaison between directors and administrative colleagues, ends up taking on more admin responsibilities and less consulting work; this tends to undermine their credibility in the firm.

In law, the biggest hurdle is always gaining partnership:

For a lawyer to become partner he or she has to be extremely good. They have to reach a minimum high standard that usually takes 8 to 10 years post qualification. Once you have proved your metal as a lawyer and made it to partner, then to become a senior partner you have to first, be interested in going down that route; many, including me, are not. Second, you have to be a good manager, have people skills, and gain the right capabilities.

He reminds us that lawyers are really pussycats:

Leading or managing lawyers is like herding cats. You have to be one of them so that you gain their respect and understand the issues lawyers face. Our current leaders were both very successful practice lawyers.

The UK head of an international architecture firm agrees:

To be a director or leader within an architecture practice you have to both maintain your competence as an expert, and importantly, be credible with both your peers and clients. This is difficult, especially when the practice is as big as ours. I think we are only now beginning to address this challenge—of having architects who can both keep up with their professional knowledge and expertise and also lead and manage a large practice.

We have been discussing whether we should have professional managers, but the trouble is they will lack the credibility as a professional to motivate their peers. My peers do not respect me because I am a good manager or leader; they respect me for my skills as an architect.

These statements raise the recurrent problem of how to combine expert knowledge with running a successful practice. Good training is viewed by some as key. For example:

Consultants are like academics insofar as they are people who carry a particular expertise and knowledge. Individuals who excel in one area are not necessarily competent in all other areas, so management training is therefore very important even for established experts. Consultants not only have to attract business but they are also required to manage client relations and quite large teams of people. We tend to use former consultants who have become specialist management trainers. They know the world of consulting, and understand the managerial weak spots of experts.

The lawyer I spoke with explained that his firm prides itself on offering very good service to clients. Thus they use training a great deal, in particular:

We offer training to those who want to go into management and leadership, for example Harvard offers a great course.

The lack of management training for those qualifying as professionals and experts was also raised in this interview:

Architecture is not alone. When most professionals and experts are educated at university it tends to be devoid of any management training. Then as people become architects they still are unprepared for any management roles. I learned leadership on the hoof by being in an architecturally related management position. Eventually I did a course at Harvard.

Consulting firms, which are somewhat less specialized than law or architecture firms, have a slightly different approach. In an interview:

We practice leadership at every level. We start developing leadership in our junior staff fairy early, both through practical experience—for example, they may lead a small team on an audit—and also through training opportunities. Client work defines our business. Management is an intrinsic part of engaging with clients. We differ from lawyers, say, where only a few will chose the senior partner route. In general, lawyers are more specialized. We first train incoming graduates as accountants, and then more broadly in management.

Experts are defined by their knowledge. They are beneficial to their organizations when they apply and develop that knowledge. A conflict is created when the drilling-down required of the expert clashes with the vertical or big-picture perspective needed by someone who leads. The head of one of the largest consulting firms explained to me that professional service firms often recognize individuals who are both interested in combining their expert practice with a leadership role and competent to do so. His firm had recently adopted a new approach:

> We have started to identify around 100 people to fast-track as potentials for senior management roles. I had mixed feelings about this at first, because I feared that the other 14,500 people might feel left out. In fact, the 100 have responded very well and there does not appear to be any negative reactions from others.

Although limited, the interview material presented above suggests the need for leaders in professional service firms to be respected experts in their given field. Nevertheless, as with university presidents, expert leaders must not be incompetent managers.

This suggested requirement, for a leader to be identified as among the top experts in a given consultancy, law firm, or university, may be a factor particularly helpful to knowledge-based industries; although, arguably, the same rule might also apply to the selection of chief executives in manufacturing or retailing. For example, Stuart Rose, the much admired CEO of UK chain store Marks & Spencer (M&S), has spent almost his entire career in retail, as has Lee Scott, president and CEO of Wal-Mart Stores, the world's largest retailer, and there are no doubt many other examples.[9] It is clear from the biographies of Rose and Scott that they developed their careers, and presumably their knowledge of retailing, by staying close to the sector—and some might suggest, by becoming experts.

In autumn 2008, as this book was being finished off, the world's banking sector appeared to be failing. Governments around the globe drew on large amounts of public money to recapitalize, or quasi-nationalize, private banks. Could the collapse of banks and financial institutions partly be a reflection of the sector's reliance on managers—"risk managers" instead of "risk experts"? One author, who sounded an early alarm, argued that risk manage-

---

[9] Stuart Rose began his career in retail at Marks & Spencer in 1972 before going on to the Burton Group. He was chief executive of Argos and later became chief executive of Booker. Before rejoining Marks & Spencer as chief executive, Rose was CEO of Arcadia Group. Interestingly, Lee Scott, president and CEO of Wal-Mart Stores, has remained with the same company for nearly thirty years. This is a somewhat unusual phenomenon today.

ment decisions should have been made based on expert judgment and subjective assessment. Instead, he suggests, banks assessed risks using complex
and often-inaccurate mathematical instruments, many of which were not
understood by bank CEOs or even their regulators.[10]

WHAT ABOUT LEADERSHIP IN THE ARTS?

The conductor Valery Gergiev has been called "one of the finest musicians
of the late 20th century."[11] He is artistic and general director of the Mariinsky Theatre and Kirov Opera and Ballet companies in St. Petersburg, Russia.
"Under his leadership, the Mariinsky has become one of the most cele-
brated—and recorded—opera companies in the world."[12] He is an acclaimed
artist who has gone into leadership. Gergiev is described as being a hands-
on leader insofar as he is involved in casting at many levels; he also takes
part in fund-raising and the development of the theater's physical site; and
he often attends world tours. He says, "My greatest achievement at the Mariinsky has been leadership." Gergiev, has, by his own admission, been a strong
head who does not favor democratic voting: "Democracy is not a good thing
when it comes to music. When everybody is right, nobody is right. You
cannot vote for the right dynamics or the right tempo."[13] Gergiev is a person
of energy and perseverance. Could the artistic success of the Mariinsky Theatre be attributable, in part, to the previous artistic success of its leader?

Another conductor I interviewed believes that the quality of orchestras
can be directly and substantially attributed to the quality of their artistic
directors.[14] He suggested in interview that, in a hypothetical ranking of
UK orchestras, one would likely find a link between the position of the
orchestra in the ranking, and the artistic quality of the principal conductor
and artistic director.

What about art galleries? Does it matter to the performance of a gallery
if the head has any deep knowledge of art, or are strong managerial and
leadership qualities alone adequate?

As explained by a producer in the television industry, the "creatives versus
managers" debate has been evident in that medium for a number of years:[15]

---

[10] See *Plight of the Fortune Tellers* by Riccardo Rebonato (2007).

[11] The *Guardian*, February 1998.

[12] *New Yorker*, April 1998.

[13] General information and both quotations have come from http://www.deccaclassics.-
com/artists/gergiev/gergievthegreat.html

[14] Paul McGrath is director of music at the University of Warwick and formerly associate
conductor to the Royal Philharmonic Orchestra (see appendix 1).

[15] For an interesting book on management in the creative industries—film, music, design, and fashion—see Bilton (2007).

Producers make programs, films, etc. On the whole I would say that they are more creative than they used to be. You don't have to have been a director to produce, but the majority have directed. You could be an accountant and start your own production company. But it really helps as a producer if you can understand the creative process, and also if you have worked as a director or part of the creative team: the accumulated knowledge both gives you credibility and helps one understand the market.[16]

CONCLUDING COMMENTS

Whether organizations like art galleries, museums, orchestras, and film companies ought to be led by experts is an empirical question that has not been studied in detail in this book. Instead, I have tried to raise questions that future research might address. In professional service firms, however, the evidence from the interviews and the literature is suggestive: to lead you should first have been a knowledgeable lawyer, consultant, or architect. Basketball coaches appear to benefit from having prior playing experience. Here real data are available. The findings, presented earlier in the chapter in graphs and a bar diagram, reveal that among a sample of professional basketball coaches, the better the person was as a player, the more that person succeeds as a coach approximately twenty years later. A team's performance improves within a year of a talented coach arriving at the club.

[16] John Silver was interviewed when he was head of features at Shine TV, a production company (see appendix 1).

CHAPTER EIGHT
IN CONCLUSION

RESEARCH UNIVERSITIES SHOULD BE LED by brilliant scholars, not merely talented managers. That, at its simplest, is this book's underlying message. In proposing it, I have drawn upon qualitative evidence from interviews with heads of some of the world's best-known universities, and upon quantitative evidence of various kinds. My focus has been on research universities, but the message of the book may be a wider one. In a range of settings in which knowledge is central to an organization, it will often be desirable to let experts, not expert managers, be at the helm. This is partly because over decades those experts have acquired a deep, inherent, instinctive understanding of the core business.

One possible reader of this book is a social-science researcher in the field of management. As has been pointed out elsewhere in the literature,[1] leadership research is unfashionable in business schools. Yet the topic is, I believe, important, and it attracts a great deal of interest. There are many books on leadership.[2] Anecdotes are common, the implication sometimes being that every leadership experience is different. Few empirical patterns are provided in these books. The evidence in this study, and other recent work,[3] appears to suggest that objective methods can be applied to research on leaders. There are measurable patterns that can advance our understanding about a group of people who make the most important decisions in their organizations and beyond. My hope is that management scholars, and economists, will find ideas of methodological and substantive interest within the book. Given that the focus of this study is on universities, educationalists may be interested in this work.

A second potential receiver of this information is a politician or educational policy maker. In Western society, we have lived through a recent era of so-called managerialism. This has built upon the view that the best leaders have generic skills and are primarily efficient at organizing and managing. Inside the higher education sector, it is common to hear people say that

---

[1] See Khurana (2007).

[2] Extensive summaries of theories of leadership can be found in Yukl (2002) and Northouse (2004). Khurana (2007) looks at the history of leadership research within the broader context of management education, and how it has been taught in U.S. business schools since its inception.

[3] See for example Khurana (2002); Bertrand and Schoar (2003); Jones and Olken (2005); and Bennedsen, Pérez-González, and Wolfenzon (2007).

"our top researchers should not be distracted by administration and managing; instead, they should be left alone to do research." Such an argument, which is heard too in theaters and hospitals, sounds logical. Yet it may be incorrect. In these data, universities seem to prosper when headed by accomplished researchers.

If a top scholar is to take the top job then it is also important that she or he has the power to change things. When decision-making in universities resides with large committees, any leader will be somewhat impotent. Indeed, if power is dispersed through committees, as in many European universities, it is, possibly, less likely that a top scholar will be selected as president in the first place. One reason that universities find it hard to rise up the rankings is because to change is to endure pain. On average, a large faculty or an academic department taking part in an election for a new leader will opt for the least change, not the most. The status quo protects the status of individuals. A distinguished scholar-leader might upset the order of things.

A third possible reader is a professor. It is not the job of this book to convince scholars to become leaders. But I hope I have been successful in making a case for what can happen if and when researchers lead universities. It would be unwise for professors to look down on the role of university presidents, and it may even be dangerous for the academy itself not to encourage and train a flow of talented people who wish to take leadership positions.

A fourth kind of reader is a chair of university governors. The book's practical advice is easily stated: first, appoint a leader who is among the top echelon of the experts or professionals within a given organization; second, ensure that the new head is selected with an eye on your institution's long-term strategy (and if you do not have one, why not?).

The interviews with professionals in the penultimate chapter suggest that law and consulting firms behave differently from universities. Management training and succession planning are more prevalent. Possibly this is because professional service firms are more collegial than research universities. In partnerships, professionals are legally tied into the firm in a way that academics rarely are in universities. Corporate commitment is less common among scholars, who have no share-options or similar financial packages.[4] Young academics are normally devotees of their discipline rather than their institution. After all, it is their disciplinary peers who will judge them on their publications, promotions, and grant applications. Universities may be able to learn from how professional firms behave.

Headhunters and recruiters might also read this book. Trying to identify potential organizational leaders is challenging—particularly in universities, where so many academics prefer investigation over administration. Although

---

[4] The exception might be an Intellectual Property (IP) contract.

the book advocates the selection of top scholars as leaders, it is important to avoid the convenient error of believing that all good scholars might be management or leadership material. As mentioned in the book's preface, these abilities are likely to be somewhat normally distributed among all trades people and professionals. Thus, scholars must first cut their mustard with a proven track record as managers and leaders in other academic settings. Every president and vice chancellor included in the book's dataset held a deputy position of provost, dean, or head of a major research center prior to taking the top job.

A final potential reader is a head of a research funding body or of the appointments committee to such a body. Having presidents, rectors, and vice chancellors who are scholars is important for the quality of research in a single university, and therefore, the quality of higher education in a country. If the standard of a few institutions starts to decline, the effect can snowball, and it can take years for excellence to return. The dwindling number of European Nobel laureates (in chapter 2 and appendix 4) comes to mind. The United States increased its early stock of Nobels by encouraging top scientists from Europe to move to its universities in the postwar period. These days, Nobel winners are typically born in the United States. Over the next fifty years, Nobel Prizes may well go eastward. China is investing heavily in research and higher education.[5] If we want top scholars to stay in a university, and a country, favorable conditions for them must be created.

In chapter 1, it is suggested that a president's appropriate level of scholarship will depend on where the university is—in terms of its research ambitions or position in rankings—and where it wants to be. A possible rule of thumb might be that the research success of a leader should be equal to or better than approximately the top 10 percent of faculty in the institution that a president is to lead. Using interview evidence, in the more conceptual chapter 5, I suggest four reasons why a scholar-leader might be beneficial to institutional performance: first, such leaders are viewed as more credible by those being led; second, they have a deep understanding of academe; third, scholar-leaders act as a standard-bearer for the institution; and, last, they signal to both internal and external stakeholders that research is important. Organizational strategy should dictate, as much as possible, who is chosen to lead. This suggestion might seem obvious. But the case study in chapter 6 implies that the selection process for university leaders can be arbitrary.

There is an oft-repeated claim that scholars are incapable of managing and leading. They are not. Universities are hierarchical places. Young faculty

---

[5] Currently 50 percent of China's students graduate in science or engineering subjects, compared with only 17 percent in the United States. Also, the number of researchers in those fields has equaled the United States and overtaken Japan. See University World News at http://www.universityworldnews.com.

members have to follow a standard promotion route that is mostly, but not exclusively, dependent on publications. In many disciplines, grants feed publications; they pay for experiments, surveys, or research assistants. Managing grants is an important part of most researchers' careers, as is administering teaching loads—student liaison, marking and developing communication skills for pedagogical purposes. As scholars get tenure, then professorships, and then reach mid-career, a few years as a department head is usual. It is also not uncommon for senior academics to belong to at least one university committee, and many will have become engaged in fund-raising activities. As mentioned earlier, all the university presidents in my dataset held leadership positions prior to obtaining the top job. Management activities in universities are widespread.

U.S. presidents spend a great deal of time fund-raising. Development functions are now common in UK institutions and spreading to Europe, India, and well beyond. When I visit the United States, I am sometimes told that presidents in that country are mainly fund-raisers, the implication being that they can or should do little else. The interview data suggest that this is a false impression. The U.S. university presidents interviewed made it clear that they are the strategic leaders of their institutions *and* they engage in fund-raising.

The aim of this book is to provide evidence about the kind of leader under which a research university will thrive.

Data Collection

DATA COLLECTION

Four datasets have been created for this book. They include quantitative and qualitative data. In the quantitative chapters, information has come from public sources. Qualitative data have been acquired through semistructured interviews with a number of university leaders in the United States and United Kingdom, also with members of a committee to hire a UK vice chancellor, and finally, six nonuniversity professionals.

Quantitative Data

Close to four hundred individuals are included in data presented in the statistical chapters—chapters 2, 3, 4, and 6. Data on the presidents of the world's top 100 universities (in chapter 2) were collected in October 2004. Only those presidents in post during this period are included, and to the author's knowledge no presidents changed during the time data were collected. Biographical information on the leaders came from university Web sites; on occasion, direct requests for CVs were made. Data on the 138 business school deans (in chapter 3) were collected in mid-2005. Again, information was mostly acquired through business school Web sites and requests for CVs.

Data on the 157 UK vice chancellors used in chapters 4 and 6 were collected in late 2005. The material was gathered through "Who's Who," the Association of Commonwealth Universities, and for current vice chancellors, institutional Web sites and CVs. The bibliographic data used in this study come from the Institute of Scientific Information (ISI) Web of Knowledge. Information on the Research Assessment Exercise (RAE) results came from official RAE reports published following each assessment (www.rae.ac.uk), and also from the University of Dundee's helpful Web site (www.somis.dundee.ac.uk/rae). My data are available on request.

Qualitative Data

Qualitative data consist of twenty-six interviews with leaders—both university heads and deans—in universities in the United States and the United Kingdom (see table next page), and also twelve interviews with individuals involved in hiring a vice chancellor in a UK university (who will remain anonymous). Among the primary dataset of twenty-six interview participants there are nineteen university heads, three of whom were retired. Thirteen are UK vice chancellors and six are U.S. presidents. In the case of one U.S. head, Shirley Tilghman, president of Princeton, material has been included in this book even though I did not interview her. My first working paper on this topic[1] was picked up by the *Daily Princetonian* (October 24, 2005). The Princeton-based newspaper interviewed President Tilghman and also me. This material is used in the book (the *Princetonian* article is below). Interview data with seven deans are also included. Three were deans of business schools, two in the United States and one in the United Kingdom—although one former UK vice chancellor also previously led two business schools. Finally, there were two interviews with former deans of the Faculty of Arts and Sciences at Harvard, and one with a former vice chancellor of Berkeley.

With some exceptions, interviews with leaders in the United States took place in 2005, between March and May, and UK interviews took place in 2006, between January and June. A semistructured interview method was used.

Interviews were documented by transcribing what was heard by hand into a notebook. They were not tape-recorded. I felt that university leaders would be both more candid and more at ease if a voice recorder was not used. Responses were color coded and grouped into two clusters. The first level clustered interviewees' responses around interview questions. The second level clustered interview material around the key themes that emerged from the data. In all interviews between the author and university leaders, there was an agreement that no names would be attributed to statements in any materials or publications (unless, in a few cases, approval from participants had first been sought).

In this book, no names are assigned to interview statements. Only general information—for example, "former president" or "dean"—accompanies the statements. The raw data, in the form of illustrative statements, are used to support arguments throughout the book. In chapter 5, where I present possible explanations about why leaders who are scholars might improve university performance, the main arguments have been developed out of the interview material.

In the case study, which features members of a particular UK vice chancellor's hiring committee, anonymity is given both to the institution and all panel members—as per prior agreement with participants. As part of this case study, I interviewed a number of the panel members. They included: the chair and six other members of the appointment committee, three observers from the administration, the lead headhunter, and the successful candidate (n = 12).

Finally, I interviewed five professionals: a senior lawyer, heads of two major consulting firms and a top architecture company, a TV producer, and an orchestra conductor (next page).

[1] Goodall (2006a).

TABLE A.1.1
Interviews with Leaders in Universities

INTERVIEWEE	POSITION	INSTITUTION
Derek Bok	Former President	Harvard, U.S.
Kim Clark	Dean	Harvard Business School, U.S.
Amy Gutmann	President	University of Pennsylvania, U.S.
Patrick Harker	Dean	Wharton School, University of Pennsylcania, U.S.
John Heilbron	Former Vice Chancellor	Berkeley, University of California, U.S.
Jeremy Knowles	Former Dean	Faculty of Arts and Sciences, Harvard, U.S.
Henry Rosovsky	Former Dean	Faculty of Arts and Sciences, Harvard, U.S.
David Skorton	President	Cornell University, U.S.
Lawrence Summers	President	Harvard, U.S.
Shirley Tilghman*	*President*	*Princeton, U.S.*
UK University Heads		
George Bain	Former Vice Chancellor	Queen's University, Belfast also Dean of Warwick Business School and London Business School, UK
Glynis Breakwell	Vice Chancellor	Bath University, UK
Bob Burgess	Vice Chancellor	Leicester University, UK
Yvonne Carter	Dean	Warwick Medical School, UK
Ivor Crewe	Vice Chancellor	Essex University, UK
Howard Davies	Director	London School of Economics, UK
Anthony Giddens	Former Director	London School of Economics, UK
Alan Gilbert	VC and President	Manchester University, UK
David Grant	Vice Chancellor	Cardiff University, UK
John Hood	Vice Chancellor	Oxford, UK
Paul Nurse	President	Rockefeller University, U.S.
Andrew Pettigrew	Dean	Bath School of Management, UK
Richard Sykes	Rector	Imperial College, UK
Eric Thomas	Vice Chancellor	Bristol University, UK
Nigel Thrift	Vice Chancellor	Warwick University, UK
Bill Wakeham	Vice Chancellor	Southampton University, UK

* I did not interview Shirley Tilghman; instead she was asked questions about my research by the *Princetonian* newspaper. I have used her responses from this interview in the book (next page for *Princetonian* copy).

Table A.1.2
Interviews with Nonacademics (featured in chapter 7)

INTERVIEWEE	POSITION	INSTITUTION
Maurice Dwyer	Partner	Wragge & Co.
		Wragge and Co. is a UK law firm, ranked around the 20th largest in the country.
Paul McGrath	Conductor and Director of Music	University of Warwick and formerly Associate Conductor to the Royal Philharmonic Orchestra.
Peter Oborn	Director, London Office	Aedas
		Aedas is the fourth largest architecture practice in the world.
Kieran Poynter	Chairman, London	PriceWaterhouseCoopers
		PWC is one of the world's largest management consultancies.
Graham Shuttleworth	Director, London Office Head	Nera Economic Consulting
		NERA Economic Consulting is an international firm of economists based in 20 countries.
John Silver	Head of Features	Shine
		UK/U.S. TV production company created by Elisabeth Murdoch in 2001.

* These interviews were conducted in 2007 and 2008.

Higher Education

Strong Researchers Lead Top Colleges
By Alex Gennis
Princetonian Contributor

A recent study in higher education questions the common belief that presidents of the most well known universities are chosen based on their fund-raising and leadership qualities.

The study, which will be published in the *Journal of Documentation*, instead says there is a positive correlation between "the lifetime citations of

(continued)

(*continued*)

a university's president and the position of that university in the global rankings."

President Shirley Tilghman, who was on the search committee for Princeton University's president before being nominated herself, found the results of the study consistent with what she looked for in Princeton's next leader.

"The rationale for ranking academic excellence very highly is the enormous importance we place on the president having the respect of the faculty. Without that, it is very difficult to lead a research university," Tilghman said in an e-mail. "By having an academic at the helm, the university is stating clearly what it values most highly."

I am not at all surprised by the findings in this paper. It seems entirely consistent with what I would have predicted in advance," she said.

Amanda H. Goodall, the postdoctoral researcher at Warwick Business School who conducted the study, listed several possible hypotheses to explain the correlation she found. For instance, a highly cited researcher carries symbolic significance in the eyes of faculty, or research ability might simply be a proxy for leadership and fund-raising ability.

"The best researchers might have greater inherent knowledge about the core business of the university," Goodall said.

The study found that the United States is far ahead of the rest of the world in terms of attracting the best researchers for its administrative positions.

Goodall said this might be due to the more bureaucratic style of education systems in Europe, which could put off potential leaders. Tuition at American universities also tends to be higher, she said, allowing for higher compensations for their faculty and administration.

Goodall also found that, of the 15 female presidents at the top 100 universities, six of them lead universities in the top 20. "Top universities may be more progressive in terms of hiring their leaders," she said.

The study used the number of references to the works of a particular researcher in other academic papers as the criteria for judging a president's level of academic involvement.

Goodall said she relied on peer assessment because other researchers in the field are the best arbiters of the quality of a particular person's research.

"It is very difficult to find a method of judging that is not subjective," she said.

Tilghman said she disagreed with the methodology used for ranking academic involvement.

"Counting citations is a very, very poor way to judge excellence and academic accomplishment," she said.

Appendix Two

Bibliometric Data

RESEARCH CITATIONS

Much of this book rests on the use of "citations" data. Some readers may be unfamiliar with such data. Citations are references to other people's work. In journals and books, scholarly knowledge is developed publication by publication. Older knowledge is acknowledged in current work through the writer's bibliography and references. If Dr. Z has 718 citations, that means that Dr. Z's research papers and books have been mentioned by others (that is, in others' reference lists) 718 times. Organizations like the Institute for Scientific Information (ISI, now owned by Thomson) keep track of such totals.

All the citation information used in this study comes from the Institute of Scientific Information (ISI) Web of Knowledge, the online database comprising the Science Citation Index, Social Science Citation Index, and the Arts and Humanities Citation Index. The other more recent place available for counting citations is through Google Scholar, which was not a reliable source when I started this project in 2004. Even today Google Scholar picks up citations from unpublished papers as well as published ones. ISI allows citations from published peer reviewed work only to be counted.

It is important when using citations as any kind of measure to recognize the huge differences between disciplines. For example, a highly cited social scientist might have a lifetime citation score of between 1,000 and 2,000, whereas a molecular biologist could have a score over 15,000. Bibliometric indicators have been used more consistently across the sciences, particularly in the natural and life sciences, though less so in engineering and the behavioral sciences. These disciplines publish more journal articles and have a higher prevalence of coauthorship.

The social sciences are patchier. For example, economics relies heavily on journal articles, although, unlike the science publications that tend to publish quickly, in the subject of economics it can be over two years from submission to publication. It is less common in the arts and humanities to write articles for journals: these disciplines tend more toward the publishing of books. Cronin and colleagues found that in the discipline of sociology two fairly distinct groups of highly cited academics coexisted: those highly cited through their journal articles and those through their monographs.[1] This should not present a major problem

---

[1] Cronin et al. (1997).

here because citations from both books and journals that are recorded in ISI have been counted.

Van Raan,[2] who has published a great deal on the strengths and weaknesses of bibliometrics, has raised areas for concern when using citations as measures of quality. He suggests that citation indices have become easy tools for policy makers and university administrators keen to make quick assessments of individual research output and quality. Originally the ISI system was designed to retrieve information, not to evaluate it.

Self-citing is a potential problem that can take two forms: first, overciting one's own work in academic papers and, second, self-citation in journals to try to raise a journal impact factor. An example of this is given by Fassoulaki and colleagues, where authors report a significant correlation between self-citation levels and journal impact scores in the 1995 and 1996 issues of six anesthesia journals.[3] In the top management journals, it has been argued that a kind of circularity exists, in that articles in the top journals tend to get more heavily cited for reasons beyond the actual quality of a paper.[4] This pattern likely exists across academe. For example, a young person hoping to get an article into a top journal will often be advised that it is sensible to cite other work from that journal. The top journal titles receive disproportionately high numbers of submissions; hence, almost regardless of the quality of each article, an established and famous journal is somewhat guaranteed a larger number of references. The standard of articles must of course in the long run play a part, or we would never see journals drop or rise in quality—which happens to many titles.

Other possible difficulties with citations include inconsistencies in methods of referencing and inaccuracies in citation statistics. Language biases also have been shown to exist within ISI, although it is now considered to be less of a problem because most journals publish in English. Some suggest that preferential referencing may take place in the United States (that is, that Americans are more likely to reference Americans), which may be a feature of the size of that nation's output. In a study that looks at this issue in the *Quarterly Journal of Economics*, a famous American journal, no bias is found against British and European authors.[5]

In the quantitative chapters in this book, where I use citations data, I am effectively assessing leaders late in their research careers. Van Raan notes that bibliometric measures are a more reliable indicator of scholarly influence over long periods of time. His preference for evaluating science is to couple peer review with citations. This, arguably, is becoming the norm when making new faculty appointments in research universities.

---

[2] Van Raan (1998, 2003, 2005), Van Leeuwen et al. (2001); see also Wouters (1999) and Weingart (2003, 2005).
[3] Fassoulaki et al. (2000)
[4] For recent discussion of this issue, see Clark and Wright (2007), and Judge et al. (2007).
[5] Oswald (2008).

There have been a number of studies comparing results from the UK's Research Assessment Exercise (RAE) with bibliometric measures. The RAE is heavily based on peer review. When 1992 and 2001 RAE results in three subject areas (anatomy, genetics, and archaeology) are compared with citation indicators, a strong correlation is found between the two methods of assessment. A similar correlation across all UK psychology departments in the 2001 RAE is also found.[6]

I have made an effort to try accurately to assign citation numbers to people's names. For example, I have hand counted the lifetime citations of each observation and used individuals' curriculum vitae to track career moves by comparing authors' locations assigned on academic papers. Despite this, some measurement error must be presumed. It is interesting to note there is some evidence that similar correlations have been found among studies that adopt different counting methods—those that use a very precise method on the one hand, and those where citations are assigned more approximately on the other.[7]

NORMALIZING CITATIONS TO P-SCORES

The discrepancies in citation levels across disciplines are demonstrated in the number of new cited references that appear in ISI every week. Using figures that date from October 2004, when the normalization process was developed, the sciences were generating approximately 350,000 new cited references weekly, the social sciences 50,000, and the humanities 15,000.

ISI has created a "Highly Cited" (ISI HiCi) category that identifies approximately the top 250 academic researchers (comprising less than one-half of 1 percent of all publishing researchers) across twenty-one broad subject areas for the period 1981–99. The process of recognizing HiCi's is outlined on the ISI Highly Cited Web site: "To identify Highly Cited Researchers, ISI begin with all articles indexed in the Thomson Scientific Citation Databases in a 20-year, rolling time period; the first dataset used for analysis comprised articles and their citations in the years 1981–1999, the second dataset included 1983–2002, the third dataset included 1984–2003, and upon completion, the fourth dataset will be a twenty-five-year time period, which is comprised of articles and their citations in the years 1981–2005. Each article in the data is assigned to one or more of the twenty-one categories in ISIHighlyCited.com based on the ISI classification of the journal in which the article was published."[8] The subjects are dominated by the sciences, totaling nineteen. The social sciences are also covered, but there are only two social science subject areas, namely "Economics and Business" and "Social Sciences—General." As of June 2008, no "Highly Cited" category exists for authors in the arts or humanities.

---

[6] See Oppenheim (1997), Norris and Oppenheim (2003), and Smith and Eysenck (2002).

[7] For example, comparing Seng and Willett (1995) and Oppenheim (1995).

[8] Visit www.isihighlycited.com for more information on HiCi's.

Using citation thresholds created by ISI, I have generated a normalized citation score for twenty-three subject areas. These include a score for the humanities that has been produced by me for the purposes of this study. It is necessary to note that the discipline of law is classified in ISI as being in the social sciences not the humanities. It is included here in the "Social Sciences—General" category.

Each university president is assigned a normalized citation score, which reflects both differences across disciplines and their own personal citation level. This score is referred to in the book as the P-score, which equals a president's individual lifetime citation score normalized for discipline. The P-score is used here as an exchange rate that normalizes the different citation conventions across disciplines. To create this, a president's lifetime citation score is divided by his or her subject score. The normalized P-score thus produced makes it possible to do like-for-like comparisons across individuals from different disciplines.

I have created the humanities score by using the "new cited references" generated by ISI each week. (As mentioned above the sciences approximated at 350,000 new cited references weekly, the social sciences 50,000 and the humanities 15,000.) If we divide the social science weekly score of 50,000 by the humanities score of 15,000, we get a figure of 3.33. I have then divided the "Social Sciences—General" score of 117 (see table below) by 3.33. This creates an adjusted score of 35.13. The approximate number 35 has been used here as the "Humanities, General" score.

The normalization method used in this book was created in 2004, the year the project began.

Does the Age of a Leader Matter?

This issue can be looked at from two perspectives. The first posits that older leaders have an advantage because they have had longer to accrue citations. The second argument suggests that bibliometrics are more a feature of modern academia, and through time there has been a strong rise in the number of published journals, so in this regard younger leaders are likely to have built up higher numbers of citations.

These two forces work in opposite directions.

A good first check of whether the age of a president affects his or her lifetime citation levels is to find out if older leaders have higher or lower numbers of citations. Some European universities still publish date-of-birth information, although this is not normally found on curriculum vitae. Birth dates can be loosely calculated from an individual's age at graduation from first degree. Using this method it is possible to compare the ages of presidents at the top and bottom of those in the top 100 global league table (in chapter 2). If it is shown that the top presidents are markedly older than those in the bottom 20, then adjustment of citation scores would be necessary. Because of difficulties in obtaining the age of

TABLE A.2.1
Citation Thresholds for Scientists across Different Disciplines in 2004

Subject Area	Scientist
Agricultural Sciences	154
Biology and Biochemistry	780
Chemistry	648
Clinical Medicine	1,095
Computer Science	84
Economics & Business	169
Engineering	182
Environment/Ecology	248
Geosciences	433
Humanities, General*	35
Immunology	763
Materials Science	219
Mathematics	130
Microbiology	534
Molecular Biology and Genetics	1,234
Multidisciplinary	123
Neuroscience and Behavior	908
Pharmacology and Toxicology	312
Physics	1,832
Plant and Animal Science	292
Psychiatry/Psychology	393
Social Sciences, General	117
Space Science	1,301

Citation thresholds available from Thomson at http://in-cites.com/thresholds-citation.html

* Humanities score created by Amanda H. Goodall.

* Methodology outlined above.

Note to table: The figures in the table above represent the number of citations (in 2004) that it was necessary to obtain per year to make it in to Thomson's Highly Cited category (ISI HiCi). To obtain a normalized citation score, the figure for each subject in this table is divided by the number of citations accrued by the 400 individuals in the quantitative datasets, depending on their discipline. For example, in 2004 when I hand counted Marye Anne Fox's citations (UC San Diego's president), she had 10,728. President Fox is a renowned chemist (listed as an ISI HiCi). To identify Fox's normalized citation score, I divided 10,728 by 648 (the score in the above table for chemistry), which gives her a P-score of 16.55.

presidents, only 80 percent of those in the top 20 universities (of the top 100) and 80 percent in the bottom 20 are included. The mean age of presidents in the top 20 universities is fifty-eight years. In the bottom 20 category, the mean age of president is sixty. Because of the closeness in age between these two groups, and in particular the slightly older average age of the lowest quintile, citation scores have not been adjusted.

APPENDIX THREE

The Sample of Universities
and Business Schools

TABLE A.3.1

The sample of top 100 world universities in the SJTU ranking 2004* (used in Chapter 2)

World Rank	Institution/Country	Total Score	Score on Alumni	Score on Award	Score on HiCi	Score on N&S	Score on SCI	Score on Size
1	Harvard Univ USA	100.0	98.6	100.0	100.0	100.0	100.0	60.6
2	Stanford Univ USA	77.2	41.2	72.2	96.1	75.2	72.3	68.1
3	Univ Cambridge UK	76.2	100.0	93.4	56.6	58.5	70.2	73.2
4	Univ California–Berkeley USA	74.2	70.0	76.0	74.1	75.6	72.7	45.1
5	Massachusetts Inst Tech (MIT) USA	72.4	74.1	78.9	73.6	69.1	64.6	47.5
6	California Inst Tech USA	69.0	59.3	66.5	64.8	66.7	53.2	100.0
7	Princeton Univ USA	63.6	61.0	76.8	65.4	52.1	46.8	67.3
8	Univ Oxford UK	61.4	64.4	59.1	53.1	55.3	65.2	59.0
9	Columbia Univ USA	61.2	77.8	58.8	57.3	51.6	68.3	37.0
10	Univ Chicago USA	60.5	72.2	81.9	55.3	46.6	54.1	32.7
11	Yale Univ USA	58.6	52.2	44.5	63.6	58.1	63.6	50.4
12	Cornell Univ USA	55.5	46.6	52.4	60.5	47.2	66.2	33.6
13	Univ California–San Diego USA	53.8	17.8	34.7	63.6	59.4	67.2	47.9
14	Tokyo Univ Japan	51.9	36.1	14.4	44.5	55.0	91.9	49.8
15	Univ Pennsylvania USA	51.8	35.6	35.1	61.2	44.6	72.6	34.0
16	Univ California–Los Angeles USA	51.6	27.4	32.8	60.5	48.1	79.9	24.8
17	Univ California–San Francisco USA	50.8	0.0	37.6	59.3	59.5	62.9	48.8
18	Univ Wisconsin–Madison USA	50.0	43.1	36.3	55.3	48.0	69.2	19.0
19	Univ Michigan–Ann Arbor USA	49.3	39.8	19.3	64.8	45.7	76.7	20.1
20	Univ Washington–Seattle USA	49.1	22.7	30.2	57.3	49.6	78.8	16.2
21	Kyoto Univ Japan	48.3	39.8	34.1	40.0	37.2	77.1	46.4
22	Johns Hopkins Univ USA	47.5	48.7	28.3	43.7	52.6	71.7	14.2
23	Imperial Coll London UK	46.4	20.9	38.1	46.2	39.4	65.8	44.5
24	Univ Toronto Canada	44.6	28.1	19.7	39.1	41.2	78.4	42.8
25	Univ Coll London UK	44.3	30.8	32.9	41.0	41.0	61.1	42.6
25	Univ Illinois–Urbana Champaign USA	43.3	41.7	37.4	46.2	36.0	58.2	17.8

* The world league table ranks institutions by assigning points. This can result in two or more institutions being given the same position.

TABLE A.3.1 (*continued*)

World Rank	Institution/Country	Total Score	Score on Alumni	Score on Award	Score on HiCi	Score on N&S	Score on SCI	Score on Size
27	Swiss Fed Inst Tech–Zurich Switzerland	43.2	40.3	37.0	39.1	43.2	47.1	41.5
28	Washington Univ–St. Louis USA	43.1	25.1	26.6	41.9	46.8	56.2	44.9
29	Rockefeller Univ USA	40.2	22.7	59.8	31.5	43.6	27.1	38.6
30	Northwestern Univ USA	39.5	21.8	19.3	47.9	35.8	57.2	37.0
31	Duke Univ USA	38.9	20.9	0.0	48.6	46.8	62.7	36.2
32	New York Univ USA	38.7	33.9	25.0	43.7	39.3	50.9	19.1
33	Univ Minnesota–Twin Cities USA	38.3	36.1	0.0	53.9	35.9	69.6	12.8
34	Univ Colorado–Boulder USA	37.8	16.6	29.8	43.7	38.3	47.5	27.4
35	Univ California–Santa Barbara USA	37.0	0.0	28.5	45.4	41.4	44.0	36.2
36	Univ British Columbia Canada	36.3	20.9	19.3	36.0	31.6	59.5	34.9
36	Univ Texas Southwestern Med Center USA	36.3	16.6	33.9	33.8	40.5	40.0	34.9
38	Vanderbilt Univ USA	35.1	12.6	30.2	37.1	23.8	50.2	41.7
39	Univ Utrecht Netherlands	34.9	30.8	21.4	31.5	29.9	58.1	22.1
40	Univ Texas–Austin USA	34.8	21.8	17.1	50.2	28.8	53.7	12.8
41	Univ Paris 06 France	33.9	35.7	23.9	23.1	24.7	56.7	32.6
42	Univ California–Davis USA	33.6	0.0	0.0	48.6	37.2	64.7	20.7
43	Pennsylvania State Univ– Univ Park USA	33.5	14.1	0.0	50.2	37.7	58.7	14.2
44	Rutgers State Univ– New Brunswick USA	33.4	15.4	20.4	38.1	36.1	48.2	19.5
45	Tech Univ Munich Germany	33.3	43.1	24.1	27.6	20.4	50.0	32.0
46	Karolinska Inst Stockholm Sweden	33.0	30.8	27.8	32.7	21.6	49.8	21.5
47	Univ Edinburgh UK	32.9	22.7	17.1	27.6	36.7	49.1	31.6
48	Univ Paris 11 France	32.5	33.3	34.2	21.4	21.3	46.8	31.2
48	Univ Pittsburgh–Pittsburgh USA	32.5	18.9	0.0	42.8	26.5	67.0	20.0
48	Univ Southern California USA	32.5	0.0	27.3	41.9	23.0	53.5	20.5
51	Univ Munich Germany	32.4	37.2	21.1	12.4	32.0	56.0	31.1
52	Univ Rochester USA	32.0	33.3	9.1	30.3	27.2	44.9	50.1
53	Australian Natl Univ Australia	31.9	17.8	12.9	41.0	31.4	43.6	30.7
54	Osaka Univ Japan	31.5	12.6	0.0	26.2	31.2	72.1	30.2
55	Univ California–Irvine USA	31.4	0.0	25.0	33.8	29.6	47.2	29.9
56	Univ North Carolina–Chapel Hill USA	31.2	12.6	0.0	38.1	34.5	60.5	20.3
57	Univ Maryland–Coll Park USA	31.1	25.9	0.0	40.0	33.2	54.0	17.4
57	Univ Zurich Switzerland	31.1	12.6	27.3	21.4	30.3	48.9	29.9
59	Univ Copenhagen Denmark	31.0	30.8	24.7	23.1	22.6	48.1	29.8
60	Univ Bristol UK	30.6	10.9	18.2	32.7	26.6	49.1	29.4
61	McGill Univ Canada	30.4	28.8	0.0	31.5	26.3	59.0	29.2
62	Carnegie Mellon Univ USA	30.3	18.9	30.2	32.7	17.4	38.8	34.0

TABLE A.3.1 (*continued*)

World Rank	Institution/Country	Total Score	Score on Alumni	Score on Award	Score on HiCi	Score on N&S	Score on SCI	Score on Size
63	Univ Leiden Netherlands	29.8	25.1	15.8	30.3	22.0	47.3	30.3
64	Univ Heidelberg Germany	29.7	10.9	27.7	23.1	22.1	49.7	28.5
65	Case Western Reserve Univ USA	29.6	37.2	11.8	23.1	22.2	46.1	40.6
66	Moscow State Univ Russia	29.5	51.5	34.9	0.0	8.1	58.5	28.3
67	Univ Florida USA	29.3	15.4	0.0	33.8	24.3	66.4	16.3
68	Univ Oslo Norway	29.2	25.9	34.1	19.5	17.2	42.1	28.0
69	Tohoku Univ Japan	28.8	18.9	0.0	19.5	26.1	69.3	27.7
69	Univ Sheffield UK	28.8	23.5	14.4	23.1	28.8	46.2	27.7
71	Purdue Univ–West Lafayette USA	28.7	18.9	17.1	31.5	22.1	50.5	13.8
72	Univ Helsinki Finland	28.6	18.9	18.2	15.1	23.7	56.9	27.5
73	Ohio State Univ–Columbus USA	28.5	17.8	0.0	41.0	20.6	61.3	9.6
74	Uppsala Univ Sweden	28.4	25.9	32.9	0.0	30.4	52.5	14.5
75	Rice Univ USA	28.3	21.8	22.3	26.2	23.7	30.2	44.6
76	Univ Arizona USA	28.1	0.0	0.0	31.5	37.7	56.5	18.1
77	King's Coll London UK	28.0	16.6	23.5	23.1	19.8	46.2	26.9
78	Univ Manchester UK	27.9	25.9	19.3	21.4	18.2	48.6	26.8
79	Univ Goettingen Germany	27.4	38.8	20.4	17.5	18.2	42.8	26.3
80	Michigan State Univ USA	27.0	12.6	0.0	39.1	28.4	50.5	10.5
80	Univ Nottingham UK	27.0	15.4	20.4	23.1	20.1	45.1	25.9
82	Brown Univ USA	26.8	0.0	13.9	30.3	27.9	41.4	30.4
82	Univ Melbourne Australia	26.8	15.4	14.4	21.4	19.2	53.0	25.8
82	Univ Strasbourg 1 France	26.8	29.5	22.9	21.4	21.3	35.2	25.7
85	Ecole Normale Super Paris France	26.5	47.9	25.0	17.5	18.2	29.6	25.4
86	Boston Univ USA	26.3	15.4	0.0	32.7	29.6	51.5	9.6
86	Univ Vienna Austria	26.3	25.1	15.8	8.7	22.0	54.5	25.3
88	McMaster Univ Canada	26.0	16.6	19.3	23.1	16.2	45.2	25.0
88	Univ Freiburg Germany	26.0	25.1	21.4	19.5	18.0	40.9	25.0
90	Hebrew Univ Jerusalem Israel	25.9	15.4	0.0	26.2	29.5	48.3	24.9
91	Univ Basel Switzerland	25.8	25.9	17.5	21.4	24.2	35.5	24.8
92	Lund Univ Sweden	25.6	29.5	0.0	26.2	22.0	54.0	11.2
93	Univ Birmingham UK	25.5	25.1	11.2	24.7	14.0	47.6	24.5
93	Univ Roma–La Sapienza Italy	25.5	16.6	15.8	12.4	24.3	57.4	7.9
95	Humboldt Univ Berlin Germany	25.4	29.5	21.9	8.7	14.8	49.7	24.4
95	Univ Utah USA	25.4	0.0	0.0	32.7	30.7	48.4	20.1
97	Nagoya Univ Japan	25.2	0.0	14.4	15.1	23.7	55.3	24.2
97	Stockholm Univ Sweden	25.2	29.5	30.2	17.5	14.9	35.7	15.3
99	Tufts Univ USA	25.1	18.9	17.1	19.5	19.1	40.6	29.2
99	Univ Bonn Germany	25.1	19.9	20.4	17.5	16.7	43.9	24.1

* The world league table ranks institutions by assigning points. This can result in two or more institutions being given the same position.

TABLE A.3.2

Methodology Used in SJTU Ranking 2004*

Criteria	*Indicator*	*Code*	*Weight***
Quality of Education	Alumni of an institution winning Nobel Prizes and Fields Medals	Alumni	10%
Quality of Faculty	Staff of an institution winning Nobel Prizes and Fields Medals	Award	20%
	Highly cited researchers in 21 broad subject categories	HiCi	20%
Research Output	Articles published in *Nature* and *Science**	N&S	20%
	Articles in Science Citation Index- expanded and Social Science Citation Index	SCI	20%
Size of Institution	Academic performance with respect to the size of an institution	Size	10%
Total			100%

Copyright © 2004 Institute of Higher Education, Shanghai Jiao Tong University
* Changes were made to the Jiao Tong methodology in 2005.
** For institutions specialized in humanities and social sciences such as London School of Economics, N&S is not considered, and the weight of N&S is relocated to other indicators.

TABLE A.3.3

Sample of 100 Business Schools in the *FT* MBA Ranking 2005 (in Chapter 3)

1	Harvard Business School	17	U of North Carolina: Kenan-Flagler
1	University of Pennsylvania: Wharton	18	Duke University: Fuqua
3	Columbia Business School	19	Instituto de Empresa
4	Stanford University GSB	20	University of Virginia: Darden
5	London Business School	21	University of Toronto: Rotman
6	University of Chicago GSB	22	Ceibs
7	Dartmouth College: Tuck	22	York University: Schulich
8	Insead	24	Cornell University: Johnson
9	New York University: Stern	25	University of Oxford: Said
9	Yale School of Management	26	UCLA: Anderson
11	Northwestern University: Kellogg	27	Emory University: Goizueta
12	Iese Business School	27	University of Rochester: Simon
13	IMD	29	Rotterdam School of Management
13	MIT: Sloan	30	University of Maryland: Smith
13	UC Berkeley: Haas	31	Vanderbilt University: Owen
16	University of Michigan: Ross	32	Carnegie Mellon: Tepper

TABLE A.3.3 (*continued*)

32	Georgetown University: McDonough	66	Thunderbird: Garvin
34	University of Western Ontario: Ivey	66	Washington University: Olin
35	Esade Business School	69	Chinese University of Hong Kong
36	University of Iowa: Tippie	70	University of Pittsburgh: Katz
37	HEC Paris	71	Tulane University: Freeman
37	USC Marshall School	71	Wake Forest University: Babcock
39	Lancaster U Management School	73	College of William and Mary
39	McGill University	74	Temple University: Fox
39	University of Notre Dame: Mendoza	75	Queen's School of Business
42	SDA Bocconi	76	Bradford School of Management/Nimbas
42	University of Cambridge: Judge	76	University of California, Davis
44	Boston U Management School	78	University of South Carolina: Moore
44	Hong Kong UST Business School	79	Ipade
44	Manchester Business School	79	Ohio State University: Fisher
47	Rice University: Jones	81	Concordia University: Molson
48	U of Illinois at Urbana-Champaign	82	University of Cape Town
49	Brigham Young University: Marriott	82	University of Georgia: Terry
49	Case Western Reserve: Weatherhead	84	Australian Graduate School of Management
49	Michigan State University: Broad	84	Georgia Institute of Technology
52	University of Minnesota: Carlson	86	Coppead
53	Imperial College London: Tanaka	86	University College Dublin: Smurfit
53	Warwick Business School	88	Texas A & M University: Mays
55	Pennsylvania State: Smeal	89	Tec de Monterrey: Egade
55	University of British Columbia: Sauder	90	Solvay Business School
57	University of Texas at Austin: McCombs	91	University of Durham Business School
58	Cranfield School of Management	92	Pepperdine University: Graziadio
58	Virginia Tech: Pamplin	93	Birmingham Business School
60	City University: Cass	93	Edinburgh University Management School
60	SMU: Cox	93	University of Washington Business School
60	University of Arizona: Eller	96	University of Bath School of Management
63	Melbourne Business School	97	George Washington University
64	Babson College: Olin	98	Trinity College Dublin
64	University of California at Irvine	99	Monterey Inst. of International Studies: Fisher
66	Arizona State University: Carey	100	ESCP-EAP

Table A.3.4
UK Research Universities in the Sample* (in Chapters 4 and 6)

1.	Birkbeck College, London	29.	University of Exeter
2.	Brunel University	30.	University of Glasgow
3.	City University	31.	University of Hull
4.	Goldsmiths' College, London	32.	University of Keele
5.	Herriot-Watt University	33.	University of Kent at Canterbury
6.	Imperial College, London	34.	University of Lancaster
7.	King's College, London	35.	University of Leeds
8.	London School of Economics	36.	University of Leicester
9.	Open University	37.	University of Liverpool
10.	Queen Mary and Westfield College, London	38.	Loughborough University
11.	Queen's University, Belfast	39.	University of Manchester
12.	Royal Holloway, London	40.	University of Newcastle
13.	UMIST	41.	University of Nottingham
14.	University College London	42.	University of Oxford
15.	University of Wales, Bangor	43.	University of Reading
16.	University of Wales, Swansea	44.	University of Salford
17.	University of Wales, Aberystwyth	45.	University of Sheffield
18.	University of Aberdeen	46.	University of Southampton
19.	University of Bath	47.	St Andrews University
20.	University of Birmingham	48.	University of Stirling
21.	University of Bradford	49.	University of Strathclyde
22.	University of Bristol	50.	University of Surrey
23.	University of Cambridge	51.	University of Sussex
24.	University of Dundee	52.	University of Ulster
25.	University of Durham	53.	University of Cardiff
26.	University of East Anglia	54.	University of Warwick
27.	University of Edinburgh	55.	University of York
28.	University of Essex		

* Aston University was excluded from the sample because their RAE submissions were few in number, making comparisons in performance difficult and open to inaccuracies.

APPENDIX FOUR

The Decline of Nobel Prizes in Europe

DOES THE DROP IN NOBEL PRIZE
WINNERS IN EUROPE MATTER?

The University of Chicago boasts on its web site that an extraordinary number of Nobel laureates have been faculty members, students, or researchers at some point in their careers. That number is indeed impressive at eighty-one—more than most countries have obtained.

Chapter 2 shows that the top universities in the world are overwhelmingly American. An equivalent kind of pattern is now also true for Nobel Prize winners: in chemistry, medicine, physics, and economics. The diagrams of chapter 2 (figures 2.2–2.4) make clear that the percentages of Nobel Prizes awarded in the last fifty years to individuals based in universities in eight European countries—Austria, France, Germany, Italy, Netherlands, Sweden, Switzerland, and United Kingdom—have declined substantially. This is despite the fact that up to the 1950s the proportion of prizes acquired by these nations far outweighed the numbers awarded to U.S.-located scholars. (As suggested earlier, the case of Switzerland is somewhat different because it continues to perform well given its size.)

It used to be the case that a substantial proportion of prizes went to scholars who migrated to the United States from Europe—many of whom had completed the early years of research in their own nations of origin. Although the United States continues to be the main recipient of the international brain "gain," the proportion of immigrant new laureates in the United States has noticeably reduced.[1]

Should Europe feel any shame or regret about the fall in laureates? Is it beneficial or harmful for the world to have most experts located in one country? Presumably it is good for the United States that so many of the world's top scholars are attracted there, but it is arguably a significant loss for the nations that lose them.

Improving higher education has been a priority for China. The Chinese government has established, and invested heavily in, a core of elite universities. In 1999 there were only 8 million undergraduates, by 2005 the number had increased to over 30 million, and it is predicted that by 2010 China will have more PhD engineers and scientists than the United States.[2] If China is working

---

[1] Hunter et al. (2007).

[2] Li et al. (2008). For interesting work on the presidents of research universities in China see Feng and Zhao (2007).

so tenaciously to increase its number of top scientists, why, one might wonder, is the deterioration of European Nobels not receiving top billing as an issue among EU governments?

The drop in Nobel Prizes going to scholars in European universities is, arguably, a cause for concern. This is not the place to address exactly how this state of affairs came about, but it is appropriate for the aims of this book to touch upon a few issues. One British scholar, Bruce Charlton, who has been following the UK's slide in laureates believes the problem stems, largely, from a lack competitive drive.[3]

Henry Rosovsky, the former dean of the Faculty of Arts and Sciences at Harvard, believes that the decline of European universities happened largely because they became too democratic. Using the Netherlands and Germany as examples, he focuses on the early 1970s political activism that led to parity of power between students, administrators, academics, and government.[4] Rosovsky is of the view that they lost their mission at the point power was devolved. This situation has since improved, especially in the Netherlands. It is also possible that across the continent of Europe the concept of "excellence" was, and still is, misinterpreted as "elitism." Excellence is achievable if institutions strive to be meritocratic—challenging though that can be. Yet, in contrast, some European countries operate a system that is fairly nepotistic.[5] In France, hiring practices are less competitive, in that it can be difficult to recruit academics from outside that country.

A number of scholars point to the lack of funding that European universities receive compared with their U.S. competitors. Also, too much regulation, too little financial autonomy, and perverse incentives are believed to have contributed to Europe's abating sector.[6]

A defining feature of the United States is that it has a mixed economy of higher education; private and public systems coexist. The best universities in the world are the U.S. private institutions, although there are some important public exceptions, for example, the universities of California and Michigan, among others. A number of countries, including Brazil, China, India, Mexico, and Japan, have both public and private universities. There are some private institutions in Europe (for example, Buckingham University in the United Kingdom, Nyenrode in the

---

[3] See Charlton (2007b). On the decline of economics in the United Kingdom see Machin and Oswald (2000).

[4] Rosovsky (1991). A very interesting account of this period in Germany is given by G. N. Knauer, a distinguished professor of classics, in a letter he wrote to the mayor of Berlin and the Board of Curators at Berlin's Free University in 1974, explaining why he was resigning his position there and moving to the University of Pennsylvania (Knauer [1974]).

[5] A culture of favoring inside promotions has been shown to be prevalent in the Italian system of higher education (see Perotti [2002]).

[6] See Alesina and Spolaore (2003), Jacobs and van der Ploeg (2006), Aghion et al. (2007), Veugelers and van der Ploeg (2008). For an account of the shift in scientific leadership from Europe to the United States, see Weinberg (2008b) and Waldinger (2008). For an account of trends in science in the developing world, see Weinberg (2008a).

Netherlands, Bocconi in Italy, Catholic University of Portugal, and a small number of business schools across Europe). Universities in Europe are mostly in the public sector, although publicly assisted is possibly a fairer term for those in the United Kingdom. Most American and British public research universities now fund between 70 and 80 percent of their own operating costs. This high percentage has partly motivated the decisions by a small number of U.S. research institutions to opt out of the public system and turn private.[7] Going private is also an option for some European universities, although none have put it to the test.

In the United Kingdom, government continues to cap universities' main source of income—the level of student fees. In many European countries, fees are minimal or do not exist at all, which makes universities dependent on the decisions of central and regional governments. Faculty salaries have often been capped or tied to centralized salary scales, as in France and Italy, in many German states, and to a declining degree in Scandinavian countries and the United Kingdom. Even Canada, so close to the United States, pays fairly low salaries relative to those in major American universities. If the price of Dell computers or BMWs was set by the government, who also controlled how much the business could pay its staff, it might be expected that these companies would not prosper.

Private universities have more control over their affairs,[8] and, importantly, they can offer competitive salaries. Is it a good thing that many European countries artificially curb academics' pay? Arguably, it sends a message to their populations that education, in this case higher education, is not important. Low salaries are a disincentive when trying to attract the best minds into academia; and if the best are recruited, they are more likely to leave, often for America's universities and better remuneration packages. As suggested above (and discussed further in chapter 5), the spillover effects of universities are well documented. Thus, an academic brain drain generates economic pain.

---

[7] See Ehrenberg (2005), Lyall and Sell (2005), and Bloom, Hartley, and Rosovsky (2006).

[8] In the United States very large university endowments are beginning to be taxed by state legislators. The *Financial Times* (December 5, 2008) reported that Massachusetts is to impose a 2.5 percent tax on universities with an endowment of over $1 billion. Harvard, with a $36 billion foundation, will be hardest hit. The issue of private universities accruing and often not spending large endowments has generated a lot of debate in the United States. In January 2008, Dartmouth University announced that it would eliminate tuition for undergraduates from families with incomes below $75,000, a gesture that many perceived Dartmouth chose before the state government of New Hampshire pushed them.

Analysis of All Departments
(Those Rated Top-5 in the RAE)

REDOING THE TESTING WITH A DIFFERENT
PERFORMANCE MEASURE: THOSE DEPARTMENTS
GRADED 5A*–5E IN THE UK RESEARCH ASSESSMENT EXERCISE

My research focuses on RAE scores at the very top end. This is because I believe that achieving a score anywhere in the 5 category is not sufficiently representative of quality. In submissions that gained a 5B, C, D, or E, the problem is that many individuals are excluded. Thus, these numbers may not be a fair representation of a department's overall quality. Moreover, grade inflation may be a difficulty. In later years, many RAE submissions were awarded a 5 grade. RAE data show that in my dataset grade 5s, per se, represented 30 percent of all submissions in 1996, but by 2001 the figure was up to 55 percent of the total.

Relatively few top 5s (5A*, 5B*, and 5A) were given, which is why for the book's main analysis I chose that performance measure.

To give two examples of universities in the data: in 2001 the University of Manchester submitted forty-six of its academic departments into the RAE. Of these, thirty-seven, or 80 percent, received a grade 5. Of the thirty-seven grade 5s, fourteen, or 30 percent, received a top 5 score; in the same year the University of Glasgow submitted forty-eight academic departments into the RAE. Of these, twenty-three, or 48 percent, received a 5 grade but only six departments, or 13 percent, received a top 5 rating.

STATISTICAL RESULTS

Tables A.5.1 and A.5.2 give results for the level of grade 5 submissions in 1996 and 2001. They then report the effects of the independent variables in 1992 and 1996, again allowing for a lag. In 1996 the P-score coefficient is 0.34 (t-statistic = 2.22), which is statistically significantly different from zero at the 5 percent level; and in 2001 there is a coefficient of 0.71 (t-statistic = 3.02), significant at the 1 percent level. University income is statistically significant at the 1 percent level in 1996 and 2001. There is no significant effect from the age of vice chancellor or their academic discipline in either time phase. As mentioned above, it is natural to incorporate a longer lag.

When we examine the changes in performance over time, as can be seen in table A.5.3, there is a statistically significant effect from P-score on the changes in the number of grade 5 departments between 1992 and 1996. The coefficient is 0.17 (t-statistic = 3.30) and the level of statistical significance is 1 percent. However, when we move to the next time period of 1996–2001 in table A.5.4, the P-score has a significant effect only prior to inclusion of the finance variable. This is also the case, in table A.5.5, for years 1992–2001, where P-score is significant at the 5 percent level until income is added into the regression, at which point P-score becomes weaker.

The impact of organizational revenue is likely explained by size. As pointed out above, in the case of Manchester University, one of the largest in the United Kingdom, 80 percent of departments scored somewhere in the 5s in 2001. It is, therefore, to be expected that institutional revenue will be more important in the tables reporting results for all 5 grades where the numbers of RAE submissions are considerably higher although the standards being reached are, on the whole, lower.

In the style of Granger causality, when I run a regression using, as a dependent variable, performance in all grade 5 departments in 1992 with vice chancellors P-scores in 2001, there is a positive gradient but not a statistically significant relationship. The coefficient is 0.035 (t = 0.82).

TABLES A.5.1 & A.5.2

Regression Equations Where the Dependent Variable Is the Number of Departments Graded 5A*–5E in the UK Research Assessment Exercise

(A.5.1) The Number of Grade 5 Departments in 1996				
Independent Variables	*1*	*2*	*3*	*4*
P-score of leader in 1992	0.34*	0.22*	0.21*	0.21*
	(2.22)	(2.21)	(2.07)	(2.07)
University income in 1992/93		0.13**	0.14**	0.14**
		(8.37)	(8.36)	(8.21)
Age of leader in 1992			0.12	0.09
			(0.74)	(0.52)
Discipline of leader in 1992				−1.05
				(−0.58)
R	0.09	0.66	0.67	0.68
Constant	7.82**	−4.17**	−11.00	−9.17
n = 55				

Coefficients are shown with t-statistics in parentheses; ** $p < 0.01$ * $p < 0.05$
0 = Sciences, 1 = Social Sciences and Humanities

(A.5.2) The Number of Grade 5 Departments in 2001				
	1	*2*	*3*	*4*
P-score of leader in 1996	0.71**	0.40**	0.42**	0.41**
	(3.02)	(3.38)	(3.43)	(3.34)
University income in 1996/97		0.14**	0.14**	0.14**
		(12.18)	(11.972)	(11.61)
Age of leader in 1996			0.12	0.15
			(0.69)	(0.80)
Discipline of leader in 1996				0.86
				(0.54)
R	0.15	0.82	0.81	0.82
Constant	13.47**	−2.13	−9.24	−10.98
n = 55				

Coefficients are shown with t-statistics in parentheses;   ** $p < 0.01$ * $p < 0.05$
0 = Sciences, 1 = Social Sciences and Humanities

Tables A.5.3, A.5.4, and A.5.5
Regression Equations Where the Dependent Variable Is the Change in the Number of Departments Graded 5A*–5E in the UK Research Assessment Exercise

(A.5.3) The Changes in Grade 5 Departments between 1992 and 1996				
Independent Variables	*1*	*2*	*3*	*4*
P-score of leader in 1992	0.17**	0.15**	0.14**	0.15**
	(3.30)	(3.06)	(2.96)	(3.08)
University income in 1992/93		0.03**	0.03**	0.04**
		(4.16)	(3.40)	(4.40)
Age of leader in 1992			−0.17	−0.16
			(−1.52)	(−2.05)
Discipline of leader in 1992				−1.57
				(−1.84)
R	0.17	0.43	0.46	0.50
Constant	2.80**	−0.13	6.62	9.37*
n = 55				

Coefficients are shown with t-statistics in parentheses;   ** $p < 0.01$ * $p < 0.05$
0 = Sciences, 1 = Social Sciences and Humanities

(A.5.4) The Changes in Grade 5 Departments between 1996 and 2001

	1	2	3	4
P-score of leader in 1996	0.23*	0.14	0.14	0.12
	(2.06)	(1.28)	(1.22)	(1.11)
University income in 1996/97		0.04**	0.04**	0.03**
		(3.45)	(3.28)	(3.03)
Age of leader in 1996			0.08	0.14
			(0.46)	(0.85)
Discipline of leader in 1996				2.11
				(0.15)
R	0.74	0.28	0.27	0.31
Constant	6.13**	2.62	−1.47	−5.70
n = 55				

Coefficients are shown with t-statistics in parentheses: ** $p < 0.01$ * $p < 0.05$
0 = Sciences, 1 = Social Sciences and Humanities

(A.5.5) The Changes in Grade 5 Departments between 1992 and 2001

	1	2	3	4
P-score of leader in 1992	0.26*	0.16	0.16	0.16
	(2.18)	(1.59)	(1.50)	(1.49)
University income in 1992/93		0.09**	0.09**	0.09**
		(5.45)	(5.20)	(5.05)
Age of leader in 1992			−0.11	−0.12
			(−0.69)	(−0.71)
Discipline in 1992				−0.34
				(−0.18)
R	0.08	0.46	0.47	0.47
Constant	9.51**	2.32	8.85	9.44
n = 55				

Coefficients are shown with t-statistics in parentheses; ** $p < 0.01$ * $p < 0.05$
0 = Sciences, 1 = Social Sciences and Humanities

APPENDIX SIX

Notes from a Department Head

MARK HARRISON'S SURVIVAL
GUIDE FOR DEPARTMENT CHAIRS

Disclaimer. These Are Some of the Things I Wish I Had Done, Not the Things I Did.

1. Search out talent. Your first priority is to bring the best people in the world that you can to your department and try to hire them. If this takes up less than half your time, you may not be putting first things first. Your department *is* the people that you and your predecessors hired. The people that you hire will have a more lasting impact on your department than anything else you do.

2. Take responsibility for others' failures, not their successes. Some of those around you may lack confidence in their own leadership and administrative competence. Expecting to fail, they will give time to self-insurance and setting up reasons for failure. Confident that you will take responsibility if things go wrong, they will switch effort from insurance to their core tasks; their work will become more productive and more likely to succeed. This is one secret of building a team.

3. Appear to be in control at all times. Smile a lot, and remain calm no matter how extreme the circumstances. If you do this, people will believe that you are in charge, and they will behave accordingly. If you stop pretending, even for a moment, people will say that you are losing it. And you will have lost their confidence.

4. Respect process. Quick decisions are good, and process takes time. But process permits consultation, ownership, and legitimacy. If your department has clear processes, for example, for probation or promotion, uphold them. If your department lacks them, devise them, have them agreed, and be bound by them yourself.

5. Manage your manager. Sometimes, you will need to take a decision to the vice chancellor, president, or dean. Remember that these people are just as overworked as you are. If possible, never go to them without being able to state clearly what is the outcome that you prefer and why that outcome is best. Your bosses will not only give you what you want but will be grateful to you because you solved their problem before they knew it existed.

6. Maintain good relations with everyone. You never know when you will need an ally or someone to cover your back. Do not pick fights unnecessarily. If you find you have done so, apologize at once, then try to make amends.

7. Don't hide behind e-mail. Walk down the corridor and knock on a door rather than send an e-mail twenty meters. If you have a hard message to deliver, give it bluntly, face to face. Don't let e-mail rush you or panic you. If an e-mail gets under your skin, wait 24 hours; preferably, don't reply; if you must, reply in person. If you gave offense by e-mail, apologize in person.

8. Tell the students what you are going to do, before you do it; then, do it. This is the first of two minimum requirements of civilized behavior that you must enforce on your colleagues—and maintain yourself—at all costs.

9. The other is: Do not make the support staff cry. For that, no one is too important to be made to apologize. Remember that chairs come and go. Your support staff will still be running your department long after you are gone.

10. Spend as much as you can. A financial surplus never made a great department. However, financial losses can ruin a department, so you must have enough income to spend it.

11. Spend as much as you can on food. The larger your department, the more it needs to be fed. Food brings people together and keeps them cheerful. They will enjoy each other's company, and rediscover what they share.

12. Give something back to the underprivileged. Occasionally, spend time with your family and former friends.

Finally, it is *your* department. Own it with pride.

References

Adams, J. D. (1990). Fundamental Stocks of Knowledge and Productivity Growth. *Journal of Political Economy* 98: 673–702.

Adams, J. D., G. C. Black, J. R. Clemmons, and P. E. Stephan (2005). Scientific Teams and Institutional Collaborations: Evidence from US universities, 1981–1999. *Research Policy* 34 (3): 259–85.

Adams, J. D., and J. R. Clemmons (2008). The Origins of Industrial Scientific Discoveries. National Bureau of Economic Research, Working Paper 13823.

Aghion, P. (2006). A Primer on Innovation and Growth. Bruegel Policy Brief 6, 1–8.

Aghion, P., L. Boustan, C. Hoxby, and J. Vandenbussche (2005). Exploiting States' Mistakes to Identify the Causal Impact of Education on Growth. Harvard Working Paper.

Aghion, P., M. Dewatripont, C. Hoxby, A. Mas-Colell, and A. Sapir (2007). Why Reform Europe's Universities. Bruegel Policy Brief, Brussels.

Alesina, A., and E. Spolaore (2003). *The Size of Nations.* MIT Press: Cambridge, MA.

Alvesson, M. (1992). Leadership as Social Integrative Action: A Study of a Computer Consultancy Company. *Organization Studies* 13: 185–209.

Alvesson, M. (2004). *Knowledge Work and Knowledge-Intensive Firms.* Oxford University Press: Oxford.

Alvesson, M., and S. Sveningsson (2003). Good Visions, Bad Micro-Management, and Ugly Ambiguity: Contradictions of Non-Leadership in a Knowledge-Intensive Organization. *Organization Studies* 24 (6): 961–88.

Anselin, L., A. Varga, and Z. J. Acs (1997). Local Geographic Spillovers between University Research and High Technology Innovations. *Journal of Urban Economics* 42: 422–48.

Anselin, L., A. Varga, and Z. J. Acs (2000). Geographic Spillovers and University Research: A Spatial Econometric Perspective. *Growth and Change* 31: 501–15.

Aram, J. D., and P. F. Salipante (2003). Bridging Scholarship in Management: Epistemological Reflections. *British Journal of Management* 14 (3): 189–205.

Augier, M., and D. J. Teece (2005). Reflections on (Schumpeterian) Leadership: A Report on a Seminar on Leadership and Management Education. *California Management Review* 47 (2): 114–36.

Azoulay, P., J. G. Zivin, and J. Wang (2007). Superstar Extinction. National Bureau of Economic Research Working Paper.

Bargh, C., J. Bocock, P. Scott, and D. Smith (2000). *University Leadership: The Role of the Chief Executive.* Open University Press: Buckingham, England.

Barnett, R. (1988). Limits to Academic Freedom: Imposed Upon or Self-Imposed? in M. Tight (Ed.), *Academic Freedom and Responsibility.* SRHE, Open University Press: Philadelphia.

Bass, B. M. (1985). *Leadership and Performance beyond Expectation.* Free Press: New York.

Bass, B. M. (1990). From Transactional to Transformational Leadership: Learning to Share the Vision. *Organizational Dynamics,* Winter: 19–31.

Basu, S., J. G. Fernald, and M. D. Shapiro (2001). Productivity Growth in the 1990s: Technology, Utilization or Adjustment? National Bureau of Economic Research, Working Paper 8359.

Basu, S., J. G. Fernald, N. Oulton, and S. Srinivasan (2003). The Case of the Missing Productivity Growth: Or, Does Information Technology Explain Why Productivity Accelerated in the U.S. but Not in the U.K. National Bureau of Economic Research, Working Paper 10010.

Batt, R. (2001). The Economics of Teams among Technicians. *British Journal of Industrial Relations* 39 (1): 1–25.

Becker, G. S. (1964). *Human Capital: A Theoretical and Empirical Analysis, with Special Reference to Education.* University of Chicago Press: Chicago.

Becker, G. S. (1973). A Theory of Marriage: Part I. *Journal of Political Economy* 81 (4): 813–46.

Bence, V. and C. Oppenheim (2004). A Comparison of Journal Submissions to the UK's Research Assessment Exercises 1996 and 2001 for UoA 43 (Business and Management). *European Management Journal* 22 (4): 402–17.

Bennedsen, M., F. Pérez-González, and D. Wolfenzon (2007). Do CEOs Matter? Copenhagen Business School, Working Paper.

Bennis, W. G. (1989). *On Becoming a Leader.* Hutchinson Business Books: London.

Bennis, W. G., and B. Nanus (1985). *Leaders.* Harper and Row: New York.

Bennis, W. G., and J. O'Toole (2005). How Business Schools Lost Their Way. *Harvard Business Review* 83 (5): 96–104.

Bensimon, E. M. (1989). Five Approaches to Think About: Lessons Learned from Experienced Presidents, in E. M. Bensimon, M. Gade, and J. Kauffman (Eds.), *On Assuming a College or University Presidency.* American Association for Higher Education: Washington, DC.

Bertrand, M., and A. Schoar (2003). Managing with Style: The Effect of Managers on Firm Policies. *Quarterly Journal of Economics* 118: 1169–1208.

Bessant, J., S. Birley, C. Cooper, S. Dawson, J. Gennard, M. Gardiner, A. Gray, P. Jones, C. Mayer, J. McGee, M. Pidd, G. Rowley, J. Saunders, and A. Stark (2003). The State of the Field in UK Management Research: Reflections of the Research Assessment Exercise (RAE) Panel. *British Journal of Management* 14 (1): 51–68.

Bilton, C. (2007). *Management and Creativity.* Blackwell Publishing: Oxford.

Birnbaum, R. (1988). *How Colleges Work: The Cybernetics of Academic Organization and Leadership.* Jossey-Bass: San Francisco.

Birnbaum, R. (1992). *How Academic Leadership Works: Understanding Success and Failure in the College Presidency.* Jossey-Bass: San Francisco.

Birnbaum, R., and P. D. Umbach (2001). Scholar, Steward, Spanner, Stranger: The Four Career Paths of College Presidents. *Review of Higher Education* 24 (3): 203–17.

Bloom, D. E., M. Hartley, and H. Rosovsky (2006). Beyond Private Gain: The Public Benefits of Higher Education, in J. J. F. Forest and P. G. Altbach (Eds.), *International Handbook of Higher Education*, 293–308. Springer: Dordrecht, Netherlands.

Bok, D. (2003). *Universities in the Marketplace: The Commercialization of Higher Education*. Princeton University Press: Princeton, NJ.

Bornstein, R. (2003). *Legitimacy in the Academic Presidency: From Entrance to Exit*. Praeger: Westport, CT.

Bowen, W. G. (1994). *Inside the Boardroom: Governance by Directors and Trustees*. Wiley: New York.

Bowen, W. G. (2008). *The Board Book: An Insider's Guide for Directors and Trustees*. Norton: New York.

Bowen, W. G., and H. T. Shapiro (Eds.) (1998). *Universities and Their Leadership*. Princeton University Press: Princeton, NJ.

Bramwell, A., and D. A. Wolfe (2008). Universities and Regional Economic Development: The Entrepreneurial University of Waterloo. *Research Policy*, published online June, doi:10.1016/j.respol.

Breakwell, G. M., and M. Y. Tytherleigh (2007). UK University Leaders at the Turn of the 21st Century: Changing Patterns in Their Socio-Demographic Characteristics. *Higher Education* 56 (1): 109–27.

Brodie, H. K. H., and L. Banner (2005). *The Research University Presidency in the Late 20th Century*. American Council on Education and Praeger: Westport, CT.

Bryman, A., M. Stephens, and C. Campo (1996). The Importance of Context: Qualitative Research and the Study of Leadership. *Leadership Quarterly* 7 (3): 353–70.

Carnegie Foundation for the Advancement of Teaching (1994). *A Classification of Institutions of Higher Education*. Carnegie Foundation for the Advancement of Teaching: Princeton, NJ.

Chait, R. P., T. P. Holland, and B. E. Taylor (1991). *The Effective Board of Trustees*. Macmillan: New York.

Chait, R. P., T. P. Holland, and B. E. Taylor (1996). *Improving the Performance of Governing Boards*. ACE/Onyx: Phoenix, AZ.

Chait, R. P., W. P. Ryan, and B. E. Taylor (2005). *Governance as Leadership: Reframing the Work of Nonprofit Boards*. John Wiley and Sons: Hoboken, NJ.

Chamorro-Premuzic, T., A. Furnham, A. N. Christopher, J. Garwood, and G. N. Martin (2008). Birds of a Feather: Students' Preferences for Lecturers' Personalities as Predicted by Their Own Personality and Learning Approaches. *Personality and Individual Differences* 44 (4): 965–76.

Charlton, B. G. (2002). Audit, Accountability, Quality, and All That: The Growth of Managerial Technologies in UK Universities, in S. Prickett and P. Erskine-Hill (Eds.), *Education! Education! Education! Managerial Ethics and the Law of Unintended Consequences*. Imprint Academic: Thorverton, England.

Charlton, B. G. (2007a). Scientometric Identification of Elite "Revolutionary Science" Research Institutions by Analysis of Trends in Nobel Prizes, 1947–2006. *Medical Hypotheses* 68: 931–34.

Charlton, B. G. (2007b). Why There Should Be More Science Nobel Prizes and Laureates—and Why Proportionate Credit Should Be Awarded to Institutions. *Medical Hypotheses* 68: 471–73.

Clark, A. E., and A. J. Oswald (1996). Satisfaction and Comparison Income. *Journal of Public Economics* 61: 359–81.

Clark, T., and M. Wright (2007). Reviewing Journal Rankings and Revisiting Peer Reviews: Editorial Perspectives. *Journal of Management Studies* 44 (4): 612–21.

Clarke, J., and J. Newman (1994). The Managerialisation of Public Services, in J. Clarke, A. Cochrane, and E. McLaughlin (Eds.), *Managing Social Policy.* Sage: London.

Clarke, J., and J. Newman (1997). *The Managerial State: Power, Politics, and Ideology in the Remaking of Social Welfare.* Sage: London.

Cohen, M. D., and J. G. March (1974). *Leadership and Ambiguity.* McGraw-Hill: New York.

Cohen, W. M., R. R. Nelson, and J. P. Walsh (2002). Links and Impacts: The Influence of Public Research on Industrial R&D. *Management Science* 48: 1–23.

Collison, P., and J. Millen (1969). University Chancellors, Vice Chancellors, and College Principals: A Social Profile. *Sociology* 3 (1): 77–109.

Cornforth, C. (Ed.) (2005). *The Governance of Public and Non-Profit Organisations: What Do Boards Do?* Routledge: London.

Cronin, B., H. Snyder, and H. Atkins (1997). Comparative Citation Rankings of Authors in Monographic and Journal Literature: A Study of Sociology. *Journal of Documentation* 53 (3): 263–73.

Datta, D. K., and J. P. Guthrie (1994). Executive Succession: Organizational Antecedents of CEO Characteristics. *Strategic Management Journal* 15 (7): 569–77.

Deem, R. (1998). New Managerialism in Higher Education: The Management of Performances and Cultures in Universities. *International Studies in the Sociology of Education* 8 (1): 47–70.

Deem, R., and K. J. Brehony (2005). Management as Ideology: The Case of "New Managerialism" in Higher Education. *Oxford Review of Education* 31 (2): 217–35.

Deem, R., S. Hillyard, and M. Reed (2007). *Knowledge, Higher Education, and the New Managerialism: The Changing Management of UK Universities.* Oxford University Press: Oxford.

Dewan, T., and D. P. Myatt (2008). The Qualities of Leadership: Direction, Communication, and Obfuscation. *American Political Science Review* (102): 351–68.

Dolton, P., and A. Ma (2001). *CEO Pay in the Public Sector: The Case of Vice Chancellors in UK Universities.* Newcastle University Discussion Papers in Economics.

Dossabhoy, N. S., and P. D. Berger (2002). Business School Research: Bridging the Gap between Producers and Consumers. *Omega-International Journal of Management Science* 30 (4): 301–14.

Ehrenberg, R. G. (2002). Studying Ourselves: The Academic Labor Market—Presidential Address to the Society of Labor Economists (Baltimore, May 3). *Journal of Labor Economics* 21 (2): 267–87.

Ehrenberg, R. G. (2005). The Perfect Storm and the Privatization of Public Higher Education. Cornell Higher Education Research Institute Working Paper, Cornell University.

Ehrenberg, R. G. (Ed.) (2004). *Governing Academia.* Cornell University Press: Ithaca, NY.

Ehrenberg, R. G., J. J. Cheslock, and J. Epifantseva (2001). Paying Our Presidents: What Do Trustees Value? *Review of Higher Education* 25 (1): 15–37.

Fassoulaki, A., A. Paraskeva, K. Papilas, and G. Karabinis (2000). Self-Citations in Six Anaesthesia Journals and Their Significance in Determining the Impact Factor. *British Journal of Anaesthesia* 87 (2): 266–69.

Feng, Z., and W. Zhao (2007). Research University Presidents, in N. Liu and L. Zhou (Eds.), *Constructing Chinese Research Universities for Achieving the Goal of an Innovative Country.* Renmin University Press: Beijing, China.

Fenton, E., and A. M. Pettigrew (2006). Leading Change in the New Professional Service Firm: Characterizing Strategic Leadership in a Global Context, in R. Greenwood and R. Suddaby (Eds.), *Professional Service Firms,* Research in the Sociology of Organizations, Vol. 24. Elsevier JAI Press: Amsterdam.

Festinger, L. (1954). A Theory of Social Comparison Processes. *Human Relations* 7:117–40.

Fiedler, F. E. (1967). *A Theory of Leadership Effectiveness.* McGraw-Hill: New York.

Finegold, D., G. S. Benson, and D. Hecht (2007). Corporate Boards and Company Performance: Review of Research in Light of Recent Reforms. *Corporate Governance—An International Review* 15 (5): 865–78.

Finkelstein, S., and D. C. Hambrick (1996). *Strategic Leadership: Top Executives and Their Effects on Organizations.* West Publishing: Minneapolis.

Freedman, J. O. (2004). Presidents and Trustees, in R. G. Ehrenberg (Ed.), *Governing Academia.* Cornell University Press: Ithaca, NY.

Galenson, D. W., and B. A. Weinberg (2000). Age and the Quality of Work: The Case of Modern American Painters. *Journal of Political Economy* 108 (4): 671–777.

Galenson, D. W., and B. A. Weinberg (2005). Creative Careers: The Lifecycles of Nobel Laureates in Economics. National Bureau of Economic Research, Working Paper 11799.

Galton, F. (1886). Regression towards Mediocrity in Hereditary Stature. *Journal of the Anthropological Institute* 15: 246–63.

Garfield, E., and A. Welljams-Dorof (1992). Of Nobel Class: A Citation Perspective on High Impact Research Authors. *Theoretical Medicine* 13 (2): 117–35.

Geary, J., L. Marriott, and M. Rowlinson (2004). Journal Rankings in Business and Management and the 2001 Research Assessment Exercise in the UK. *British Journal of Management* 15 (2): 95–141.

Glover, I. (1985). How the West Was Lost? Decline in Engineering and Manufacturing in Britain and the United States. *Higher Education Review* 17 (3): 3–34.

Goffee, R., and G. Jones (2007). Leading Clever People. *Harvard Business Review* 85 (3): 72–79.

Goldin, C., and C. Rouse (2000). Orchestrating Impartiality: The Impact of "Blind" Auditions on Female Musicians. *American Economic Review* 90 (4): 715–41.

Goodall, A. H. (2006a). An Empirical Study of Business School Deans. Cornell Higher Education Research Institute, Working Paper 89.

Goodall, A. H. (2006b). Should Top Universities Be Led by Top Researchers and Are They? *Journal of Documentation* 62 (3): 388–411.

Goodall, A. H. (2009). Highly Cited Leaders and the Performance of Research Universities. *Research Policy*, forthcoming.

Goodall, A. H., L. M. Kahn, and A. J. Oswald (2008). Why Do Leaders Matter? The Role of Expert Knowledge. IZA Discussion Paper 3583.

Gosling, J., and H. Mintzberg (2004). Agenda: The Education of Practicing Managers. *MIT Sloan Management Review* 45 (4): 19–22.

Granger, C. W. J., and P. Newbold (1974). Spurious Regressions in Econometrics. *Journal of Econometrics* 2: 111–20.

Greatrix, P. (2005). *Dangerous Medicine: Problems with Assuring Quality and Standards in UK Higher Education.* Warwick University Press: Warwick, England.

Hallock, K. (2002). Managerial Pay and Governance in American Nonprofits. *Industrial Relations* 41 (3): 377–406.

Halsey, A., and M. Trow (1971). *The British Academics.* Faber and Faber: London.

Hambrick, D. C., and P. Mason (1984). Upper Echelons: The Organization as a Reflection of Its Top Managers. *Academy of Management Review* 9: 193–206.

Hamermesh, D. S., G. E. Johnson, and B. A. Weisbrod (1982). Scholarship, Citations, and Salaries: Economic Rewards in Economics. *Southern Economic Journal* 49 (2): 472–81.

Hammond, T. H. (2004). Herding Cats in University Hierarchies, in R. G. Ehrenberg (Ed.), *Governing Academia.* Cornell University Press: Ithaca, NY.

Handy, C. (1984). Education for Management outside Business, in S. Goodlad (Ed.), *Education for the Professions.* Society for Research into Higher Education and NFER-Nelson: Guildford, England.

Hardin, C. D., and E. T. Higgins (1996). Shared Reality: How Social Verification Makes the Subjective Objective, in E. T. Higgins and R. M. Sorrentino (Eds.), *Handbook of Motivation and Cognition: The Interpersonal Context*, Vol. 3. Guilford Press: New York.

Hermalin, B. E. (1998). Toward an Economic Theory of Leadership: Leading by Example. *American Economic Review* 88 (5): 1188–1206.

Hermalin, B. E. (2007). Leading for the Long Term. *Journal of Economic Behavior and Organization* 62 (1): 1–19.

Hickson, D. J., S. J. Miller, and D. C. Wilson (2003). Planned or Prioritized? Two Options in Managing the Implementation of Strategic Decisions. *Journal of Management Studies* 40 (8): 2211–17.

Hood, C. (2000). Paradoxes of Public Sector, Old Public Management and Public Service Bargains. *International Public Management Journal* 3 (1): 1–22.

Hume, D. (1967). *A Treatise of Human Nature (1888)*, edited by L. A. Selby-Bigg. Clarendon Press: Oxford.

Hunter, R. S., A. J. Oswald, and B. G. Charlton (2007). The Elite Brain Drain and Scientists' (H-Index) Productivity. Warwick University Working Paper.

Jackson, P. M. (2006). *Sarbanes-Oxley for Nonprofit Boards: A New Governance Paradigm*. Wiley: Hoboken, NJ.

Jacobs, B., and F. van der Ploeg (2006). Guide to Reform of Higher Education: A European Perspective. *Economic Policy* 47: 535–92.

Jarratt, A. (1985). Report of the Steering Committee for Efficiency Studies in Universities. Committee of Vice Chancellors and Principals: London.

Jarzabkowski, P. (2005). Strategy as Practice: An Activity-Based Approach. Sage: London.

Jenkins, S. (1995). *Accountable to None: The Tory Nationalization of Britain*. Penguin Books: London.

Jones, B. F., and B. A. Olken (2005). Do Leaders Matter? National Leadership and Growth since World War II. *Quarterly Journal of Economics* 120 (3): 835–64.

Judge, T. A., D. M. Cable, A. E. Colbert, and S. L. Rynes (2007). What Causes a Management Article to be Cited—Article, Author, or Journal? *Academy of Management Journal* 50 (3): 491–506.

Keohane, N. O. (2006). *Higher Ground: Ethics and Leadership in the Modern University*. Duke University Press: Durham, NC.

Kerr, C. (2001). *The Gold and the Blue: Volume One, Academic Triumphs*. University of California Press: Berkeley.

Kezar, A. (2006). Rethinking Public Higher Education Governing Boards Performance: Results of a National Study of Governing Boards in the United States. *Journal of Higher Education* 77 (6): 968–1008.

Khurana, R. (2002). *Searching for a Corporate Savior: The Irrational Quest for Charismatic CEOs*. Princeton University Press: Princeton, NJ.

Khurana, R. (2007). *From Higher Aims to Hired Hands: The Social Transformation of American Business Schools and the Unfulfilled Promise of Management as a Profession*. Princeton University Press: Princeton, NJ.

Kim, H., and W. Ocasio (1999). The Circulation of Corporate Control: Decline of Financial CEOs in Large U.S. Manufacturing Firms, 1981–1992. *Administrative Science Quarterly* 39: 118–40.

Knauer, G. N. (1974). The Academic Consequences of Disorder in the German Universities: Professor Knauer's Resignation from the Free University of Berlin. *Minerva* 12 (4): 510–14.

Kotter, J. (1988). *The Leadership Factor*. Free Press: New York.

Kotter, J. (1990). What Leaders Do. *Harvard Business Review* May–June: 103–11.

Kouzes, J. M., and B. Z. Posner (2003). *Credibility: How Leaders Gain and Lose It, Why People Demand It*. Jossey-Bass: San Francisco.

Krueger, A. B., and M. Lindahl (2001). Education for Growth: Why and for Whom? *Journal of Economic Literature* 39 (4): 1101–36.

Kruglanski, A. W., and O. Mayseless (1990). Classic and Current Social Comparison Research: Expanding the Perspective. *Psychological Bulletin* 108 (2): 195–208.

Lazaridis, M. (2004). The Importance of Basic Research. *Research Money* 18 (November 22).

Leavy, B., and D. Wilson (1994). *Strategy and Leadership*. Routledge: London.

Leuz, C. (2007). Was the Sarbanes-Oxley Act of 2002 Really This Costly? A Discussion of Evidence from Event Returns and Going—Private Decisions. *Journal of Accounting and Economics* 44 (1–2): 146–65.

Li, Y., J. Whalley, S. Zhang, and X. Zhao (2008). The Higher Educational Transformation of China and Its Global Implications. National Bureau of Economic Research, Working Paper 13849.

Lombardi, J. V., D. D. Craig, E. D. Capaldi, and D. S. Gater (2002). The Top American Research Universities: An Overview. *The Center* Reports, University of Florida: Gainesville.

Lombardi, J. V., D. D. Craig, E. D. Capaldi, K. R. Reeves, and D. S. Gater (2003). *The Top American Research Universities. The Center,* University of Florida: Gainesville.

Lorsch, J. W., and R. C. Clark (2008). Leading from the Boardroom. *Harvard Business Review* 86 (4): 104–7.

Lotka, A. J. (1926). The Frequency Distribution of Scientific Productivity. *Journal of the Washington Academy of Sciences* 16 (12): 317–23.

Lowendahl, B. R. (1997). *Strategic Management of Professional Service Firms*. Copenhagen Business School Press: Copenhagen, Denmark.

Lucas, R. E., Jr. (1988). On the Mechanics of Economic Development. *Journal of Monetary Economics* 22: 3–42.

Luttmer, E. F. P. (2005). Neighbors as Negatives: Relative Earnings and Well-Being. *Quarterly Journal of Economics* 120 (3): 963–1002.

Lyall, K. C., and K. R. Sell (2006). *The True Genius of America at Risk: Are We Losing Our Public Universities to De Facto Privatization?* Praeger Publishers: Westport, CT.

Machin, S., and A. Oswald (2000). UK Economics and the Future Supply of Academic Economists. *Economic Journal* 110 (464): 334–49.

Maister, D. H. (1993). *Managing the Professional Service Firm*. Free Press: New York.

Majumdar, S., and S. Mukand (2007). The Leader as Catalyst: On Leadership and the Mechanics of Institutional Change. Queens University, Canada, Working Paper 1128.

Malleson, K. (2006). Rethinking the Merit Principle in the Judicial Appointments Process. *Journal of Law and Society* 33 (1): 126–40.

March, J. G. (2003). A Scholar's Quest. *Journal of Management Inquiry* 12 (3): 205–7.

May, R. (2007). Tony Blair's Era: Good News, Bad News. *Nature* 447: 1053.

McKenna, P. J., and D. H. Maister (2002). *First among Equals: How to Manage a Group of Professionals*. Free Press: New York.

Middlehurst, R. (1993). *Leading Academics*. Open University Press: Buckingham, England.

Middlehurst, R., and L. Elton (1992). Leadership and Management in Higher Education. *Studies in Higher Education* 7 (3): 251–64.

Mintzberg, H., J. B. Quinn, and S. Ghoshal (1995). *The Strategy Process*. Prentice Hall: London.

Moed, H. F. (2002). The Impact Factors Debate: The ISI's Uses and Limits. *Nature* 415: 731–32.

Moretti, E. (2004). Social Return to Higher Education: Evidence from Cross-Sectional and Longitudinal Data. *Journal of Econometrics* 121: 175–212.

Narayanan, V. K. (2001). *Managing Technology and Innovation for Competitive Advantage*. Prentice Hall Longman: Englewood Cliffs, NJ.

Neave, G. (1988). On Being Economical with University Autonomy, in M. Tight (Ed.), *Academic Freedom and Responsibility*. SRHE, Open University Press: Milton Keynes, England.

Norris, M., and C. Oppenheim (2003). Citation Counts and the Research Assessment Exercise V—Archaeology and the 2001 RAE. *Journal of Documentation* 59 (6): 709–30.

Northouse, P. G. (2004). *Leadership: Theory and Practice*, 3rd ed. Sage: Thousand Oaks, CA.

O'Neal, D., and H. Thomas (1996). Developing the Strategic Board. *Long Range Planning* 29 (3): 314–27.

Oppenheim, C. (1995). The Correlation between Citation Counts and the 1992 Research Assessment Exercise Ratings for British Library and Information Science University Departments. *Journal of Documentation* 51: 18–27.

Oppenheim, C. (1997). The Correlation between Citation Counts and the 1992 Research Assessment Exercise Ratings for British Research in Genetics, Anatomy and Archaeology. *Journal of Documentation* 53 (5): 477–87.

Oreopoulos, P. (2007). Do Dropouts Drop Out Too Soon? Wealth, Health, and Happiness from Compulsory Schooling. *Journal of Public Economics* 91 (11–12): 2213–29.

Oswald, A. J. (2006). An Examination of the Reliability of Prestigious Scholarly Journals: Evidence and Implications for Decision-Makers. *Economica* 74: 21–31.

Oswald, A. J. (2008). Unbiased Science. Warwick University Working Paper.

Perotti, R. (2002). *The Italian University System: Rules vs. Incentives*. Paper presented at the first conference on "Monitoring Italy." ISAE: Rome.

Pettigrew, A. (1985). *The Awakening Giant: Continuity and Change in ICI*. Basil Blackwell: Oxford.

Pettigrew, A. M. (1990). Longitudinal Field Research on Change: Theory and Practice. *Organization Science* 1 (3): 267–92.

Pettigrew, A. M. (2001). Management Research after Modernism. *British Journal of Management* 12 (s1): S61–S70.

Pollitt, C. (1993). *Managerialism and the Public Services: Cuts or Cultural Change in the 1990s?* Blackwell Business: Oxford.

Potter, W. G. (1988). Of Making Many Books There Is No End: Bibliometrics and Libraries. *Journal of Academic Librarianship* 14: 238a–238c.

Power, M. (1997). *The Audit Society: Rituals of Verification*. Oxford University Press: Oxford.

Pusser, B., S. Slaughter, and S. L. Thomas (2006). Playing the Board Game: An Empirical Analysis of University Trustee and Corporate Board Interlocks. *Journal of Higher Education* 77 (5): 747–55.

Rebonato, R. (2007). *Plight of the Fortune Tellers: Why We Need to Manage Financial Risk Differently.* Princeton University Press: Princeton, NJ.

Rosovsky, H. (1991). *The University: An Owner's Manual.* Norton: New York.

Seng, L. B., and P. Willett (1995). The Citedness of Publications by United Kingdom Library Schools. *Journal of Information Science* 21: 68–71.

Shapiro, H. T. (2005). *A Larger Sense of Purpose: Higher Education and Society.* Princeton University Press: Princeton, NJ.

Shattock, M. L. (2003). *Managing Successful Universities.* Open University Press: Berkshire, England.

Shattock, M. L. (2006). *Managing Good Governance in Higher Education.* Open University Press: Berkshire, England.

Smith, A., and M. Eysenck (2002). The Correlation between RAE Ratings and Citation Counts in Psychology. Department of Psychology Working Paper, Royal Holloway, University of London.

Starbuck, W. H. (1992). Learning by Knowledge Intensive Firms. *Journal of Management Studies* 29: 713–40.

Stiles, B. L., and H. B. Kaplan (2004). Adverse Social Comparison Processes and Negative Self-Feelings: A Test of Alternative Models. *Social Behavior and Personality: An International Journal* 32 (1): 31–44.

Stuen, E. T. (2007). Academic Knowledge Spillovers Re-Examined: A Look at the Effect of Exogenous Federal Funding. Working Paper 07–05, University of Colorado: Boulder.

Suls, J., R. Martin, and L. Wheeler (2002). Social Comparison: Why, with Whom, and with What Effect? *Current Directions in Psychological Science* 11 (5): 159–63.

Swann, W. B. (1990). To Be Adored or to Be Known? The Interplay of Self-Enhancement and Self-Verification, in R. M. Sorrentino and E. T. Higgins (Eds.), *Motivation and Cognition.* Guilford Press: New York.

Szreter, R. (1968). An Academic Patriarchate: Vice-Chancellors, 1966–67. *Universities Quarterly* 23 (1): 17–45.

Taylor, W, (1986). Organizational Culture and Administrative Leadership in Universities, in T. J. Sergiovanni and J. E. Corbally (Eds.), *Leadership and Organizational Culture.* Illini Books: University of Illinois, Urbana.

Tierney, W. G. (1988). *The Web of Leadership: The Presidency in Higher Education.* JAI Press: Greenwich, CT.

Tierney, W. G. (1989). *Curricular Landscapes, Democratic Vistas: Transformative Leadership in Higher Education.* Praeger: New York.

Tierney, W., Z. Corwin, and J. E. Colyar (Eds.) (2004). *Competing Conceptions of Governance: Negotiating the Perfect Storm.* Johns Hopkins University Press: Baltimore, MD.

Tilghman, S. (2005). In *The Daily Princetonian* (October 24). Princeton University: Princeton, NJ.

Trow, M. A. (1999). Biology at Berkeley. Center for Studies in Higher Education, Working Paper CSHE1–99, University of California, Berkeley.

Trow, M. A. (2005). An American Perspective on British Higher Education: The Decline of Diversity, Autonomy, and Trust in Post-War British Higher Education. Center for Studies in Higher Education, Working Paper WP2005–3, University of California, Berkeley.

University of Warwick (2007). Elite Scientists and the Global Brain Drain. Conference paper, Shanghai Jiao Tong University.

Valenti, A. (2008). The Sarbanes-Oxley Act of 2002: Has It Brought about Changes in the Boards of Large U.S. Corporations? *Journal of Business Ethics* 81 (2): 401–12.

van Leeuwen, T. N., H. F. Moed, R. J. W. Tijssen, M. S. Visser, and A. F. J. Van Raan (2001). Language Biases in the Coverage of the Science Citation Index and Its Consequences for International Comparisons of National Research Performance. *Scientometrics* 51(1): 335–46.

van Raan, A. F. J. (1998). Assessing the Social Sciences: The Use of Advanced Bibliometric Methods as a Necessary Complement to Peer Review. *Research Evaluation* 7: 2–6.

van Raan, A. F. J. (2003). The Use of Bibliometric Analysis in Research Performance Assessment and Monitoring of Interdisciplinary Scientific Developments. *Technikfolgenabschatzung* 1: 20–29.

van Raan, A. F. J. (2005). Fatal Attraction: Conceptual and Methodological Problems in the Ranking of Universities by Bibliometric Methods. *Scientometrics* 62 (1): 133–43.

Veugelers, R., and F. van der Ploeg (2008). Reforming European Universities: Scope for an Evidence-Based Process, in M. Dewatripont and F. Thys-Clement, *Governance of European Universities*. Editions de l'University de Bruxelles: Brussels.

Waldinger, F. (2008). Peer Effects in Science: Evidence from the Dismissal of Scientists in Nazi Germany, Working Paper, London School of Economics.

Weinberg, B. A. (2008a). Developing Science: Trends in Science in the Developing World, Working Paper, Ohio State University.

Weinberg, B. A. (2008b). Scientific Leadership, Working Paper, Ohio State University.

Weingart, P. (2003). Evaluation of Research Performance: The Danger of Numbers, in *Bibliometric Analysis in Science and Research: Applications, Benefits, and Limitations*, 7–19. Second Conference of the Central Library, Forschungszentrum Jülich, Germany.

Weingart, P. (2005). Impact of Bibliometrics upon the Science System: Inadvertent Consequences? *Scientometrics* 62 (1): 117–31.

Westphal, J. D., and L. P. Milton (2000). How Experience and Network Ties Affect the Influence of Demographic Minorities on Corporate Boards. *Administrative Science Quarterly* 45: 366–98.

Westphal, J. D., and E. J. Zajac (1995). Who Shall Govern? CEO/Board Power, Demographic Similarity, and New Director Selection. *Administrative Science Quarterly* 40: 60–83.

White, P. H., and S. G. Harkins (1994). Race of Source Effects in the Elaboration Likelihood Model. *Journal of Personality and Social Psychology* 67: 790–807.

Wouters, P. F. (1999). *The Citation Culture*. PhD thesis, University of Amsterdam, Netherlands.

Yukl, G. (2005). *Leadership in Organizations*, 5th ed. Prentice Hall: Upper Saddle River, NJ.

Zalznik, A. (1977). Managers and Leaders: Are They Different? *Harvard Business Review* 55 (3): 67–78.

Zell, D. (2005). Pressure for Relevancy at Top-Tier Business Schools. *Journal of Management Inquiry* 14 (3): 271–74.

Zhang, I. X. (2007). Economic Consequences of the Sarbanes-Oxley Act of 2002. *Journal of Accounting and Economics* 44 (1–2): 74–115.

Zucker, L. G., M. R. Darby, and M. B. Brewer (1998). Intellectual Human Capital and the Birth of U.S. Biotechnology Enterprises. *American Economic Review* 88: 290–306.

INDEX

WITHDRAWAL